MAMMOTH
BOOK OF DINOSAURS

Featuring:
ICE AGE CREATURES

Modern Publishing
A Division of Unisystems, Inc.
New York, New York 10022
Printed in Italy

Introduction

Since humans have been the dominant species on Earth for such a long period of time, it is hard to imagine that other creatures existed before us. To become more familiar with these creatures, we must journey back approximately 10 thousand to 2 million years. Great Woolly Mammoths roamed in herds across continents, huge Saber Tooth cats stalked their prey and enormous Mastodons walked the Earth—these were Ice Age Creatures.

If we travel back even further in time, 100-200 million years, we enter the age of dinosaurs. This group of creatures ranges from enormous plant-eaters weighing many tons to vicious flesh-eaters with huge jaws and teeth. Some dinosaurs had leathery wings and flew; others swam in prehistoric oceans.

Then suddenly, 65 million years ago, all the dinosaurs disappeared. Scientists are still speculating on why these creatures became extinct. Although we may never know exactly why the dinosaurs disappeared, our interest and fascination with these beasts continue to grow.

This colorfully-illustrated, entertaining and fact-filled book presents a look at both of these distinctive periods of time. Adventure stories and many pages of facts bring to life both the dinosaurs and the Ice Age Creatures that followed them.

Prepare for a wonderful journey, back in time, to an Earth ruled by dinosaurs and Ice Age Creatures.

Table of Contents

Dinosaurs

Ice Age Creatures

WHAT IS A DINOSAUR?

TYPES OF DINOSAUR

There were many types of dinosaur but among the most famous was the family of sauropods. These were large, four-footed animals with small heads, long necks, large bodies, and long tails. They had quite small brains with a special nerve box in their hip to control the tail and back legs.

Heavily armored dinosaurs like this "node-lizard" ankylosaur were built for protection and combat. They walked on all fours and ate plants. Some were armed with large bony clubs at the end of the tail. Others just had side and back armor. Several types had spikes and plates.

Probably the most feared dinosaurs of all were the flesh-eating carnosaurs like *Daspletosaurus*. They walked erect on two legs; most had very small arms and weighed up to 7 tons. They could move quickly and would eat dead animals as well as kill other dinosaurs for food. All had large fangs.

DINOSAUR GROUPS

Whichever family a dinosaur belonged to it was in one of two groups. The groups were distinguished by the way their hip bones were arranged. These bones are called the ilium, the ischium and the pubis. Saurischian (lizard-hip) dinosaurs had a hip bone arrangement like that seen in the drawing on the right.

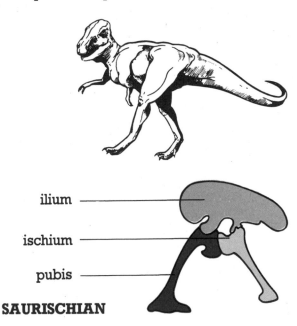

ilium

ischium

pubis

SAURISCHIAN

Ornithischian dinosaurs had the hip arrangement shown in the drawing on the left. Here, the pubis lies back along the ischium. Later, some dinosaurs had a different pubic bone shaped to point more forward than previous types and is shown here jutting beyond the ilium. All ornithischians were plant eaters.

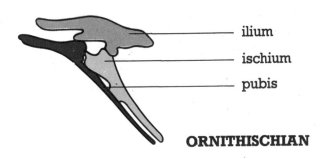

ilium

ischium

pubis

ORNITHISCHIAN

THE DINOSAUR WALK

The dinosaur was distinguished by the way its legs were attached to its hips. In the drawings below you can see the squat arrangement of a lizard, the semi-raised posture of a crocodile and the fully developed structure of a mammal or a dinosaur. The way the hip joints developed is also shown. We must not think of dinosaurs as primitive. They were highly developed.

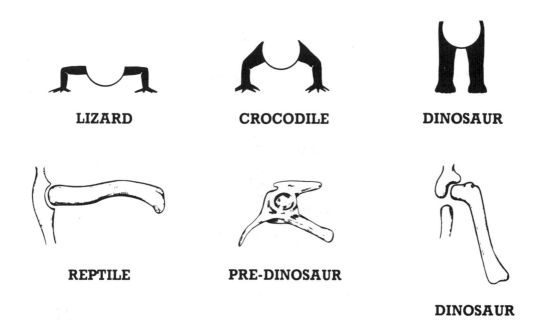

LIZARD   CROCODILE   DINOSAUR

REPTILE   PRE-DINOSAUR

DINOSAUR

DINOSAUR FEET

Some dinosaurs walked on their toes, like *Ceratosaurus* whose leg and foot is shown in the left-hand drawing below. Other dinosaur feet, like those of *Apatosaurus* at bottom right, were adapted for carrying great weights across firm ground. It is wrong to think of giant sauropods like these wallowing in marshy swamps. Studies show they would have become hopelessly bogged down!

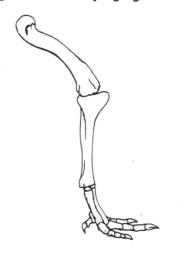

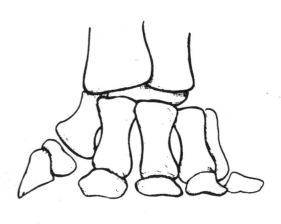

THE AGE OF THE DINOSAURS

SAURISCHIAN (LIZARD-HIP)

Dinosaurs of this type were found all over the world and lived from the middle of the Triassic period to the end of the Cretaceous. They were both meat and plant eaters, had clawed feet and included the families of sauropods (with five toes like modern lizards), carnosaurs (bipedal meat eaters) and coelurosaurs (similar to carnosaurs but with hollow bones, large brains and possibly warm blooded). Reptiles and crocodiles are shown for comparison.

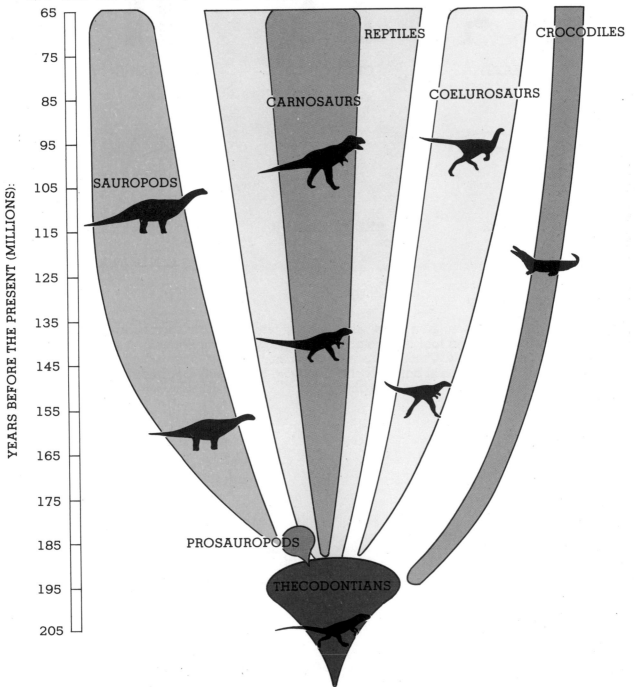

YEARS BEFORE THE PRESENT (MILLIONS):

65
75
85
95
105
115
125
135
145
155
165
175
185
195
205

REPTILES

CROCODILES

CARNOSAURS

COELUROSAURS

SAUROPODS

PROSAUROPODS

THECODONTIANS

These dinosaurs had hoofed toes, ate plants and most had beaked mouths. Some, like the stegosaurs and the ankylosaurs, had protective armor. Ornithopods were thought to have bird-like feet and ran with tails outstretched for balance. Pterosaurs were not true birds.

ORNITHISCHIAN (BIRD-HIP)

Modern birds are thought to have come from Saurischian Coelurosaurs. The age of the birds and mammals are shown for comparison. Like reptiles and crocodiles, they have survived to the present.

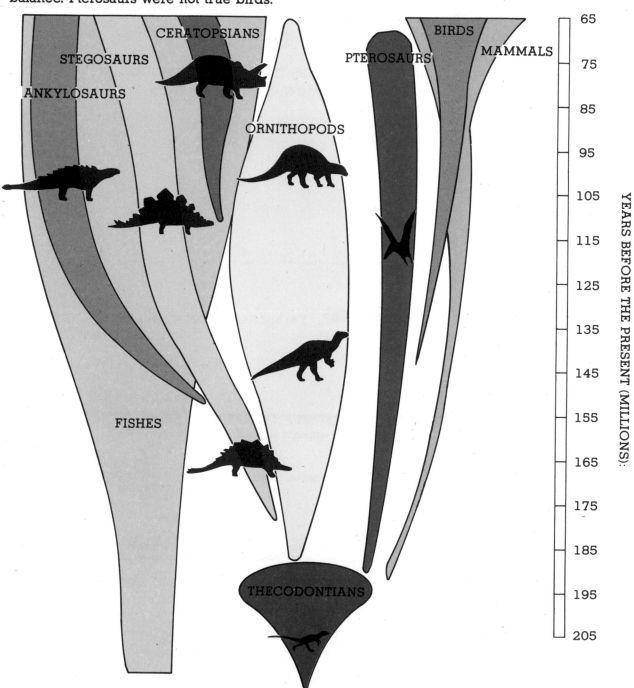

CERATOPSIANS
STEGOSAURS
ANKYLOSAURS
BIRDS
PTEROSAURS
MAMMALS
ORNITHOPODS
FISHES
THECODONTIANS

YEARS BEFORE THE PRESENT (MILLIONS):

65
75
85
95
105
115
125
135
145
155
165
175
185
195
205

THE RISE OF ICE AGE CREATURES

Two million years ago, the Earth entered the Pleistocene period which lasted until 10,000 years ago. This period is commonly known as the Ice Age.

It all began when snows on mountaintops accumulated and pressed down heavily, forming huge sheets of ice or glaciers. These sheets of ice crept down the mountains and eventually covered five million square miles of North America, in addition to sections of England, France, Germany, Scandinavia and Asia. The sheet of ice was as deep as two miles in some places.

Many animals moved south, away from the ice that was moving down from the north. Some animals became ex-

EVENT(S)

 The first SABER TOOTH cats appear.

The first MASTODONS appear.

The first
GLYPTODONS
appear

 DINICTIS—ancestor of both biting and Saber Tooth cats—appears on Earth.

 The first MAMMOTHS appear on Earth.

The PLEISTOCENE period (period of Ice Ages) begins. The first SMILODONS appear.

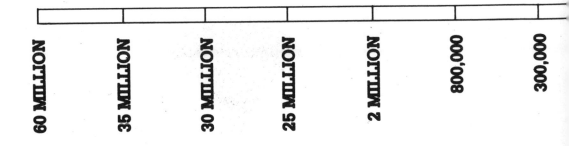

YEARS BEFORE
PRESENT TIME

60 MILLION | 35 MILLION | 30 MILLION | 25 MILLION | 2 MILLION | 800,000 | 300,000

tinct during this period due to the fact that they could not adjust to the cold climate or escape from the ice.

The Mastodon made it to the warmer climate of South America and survived for many hundreds of thousands of years. Some animals adapted, like the Mammoths who developed their woolly coats to protect themselves from the extreme cold.

The Ice Age was not a continuously long, cold period. At different intervals during the Pleistocene period, the Earth became warmer (at least four times a year). When the ice melted, new lakes would form and forests would reappear. The warm periods in between Ice Ages are known as Interglacials. Following an Interglacial, the Earth again would be covered by ice. The last Ice Age ended 10,000 years ago.

 NEANDERTHAL MAN appears in Europe.

 The end of the PLEISTOCENE period (the last Ice Age). The MASTODONS die out. AMERICAN INDIANS appear on the North American Continent.

 The first MASTODON AMERICANUS (North American Mastodon) appears.

 SQUIRRELS, BISON, and WOLVES are common, and survive to the present day.

SABER TOOTH cats die out.

 CRO-MAGNUM man appears, creating the first cave drawings and clay models.

100,000   80,000   30,000   11,000   10,000

ICE AGE CREATURES AND DINOSAUR SIZES

MASTODON

SABER TOOTH TIGER

WOOLLY RHINOCEROS

STEGOSAURUS

TRICERATOPS

COMPSOGNATHUS

From the giant Diplodocus to the tiny Compsognathus, dinosaurs came in all shapes and sizes. Here dinosaurs are compared with modern animals like the elephant, the hippopotamus, the rhinoceros, the giraffe, the dog and man. Compare the size of Tyrannosaurus with a rhinoceros and see how Triceratops would have looked to a man! Many millions of years after the dinosaurs died out, the Earth experienced the Ice Age. Thick sheets of ice reached down from the poles and covered huge areas of land. The creatures who lived during that period greatly varied in size. The Mastodon emerged about 25 million years ago and had a 10-foot-high body.

HIPPOPOTAMUS

ELEPHANT

TYRANNOSAURUS

RHINOCEROS

DIPLODOCUS

GIRAFFE

DOG

MAN

Quetzalcoatlus

Parasaurolophus

Deinosuchus

Corythosaurus

Oviraptor

18   Spinosaurus

Albertosaurus

Written by Frances Swann
Illustrated by Pam Mara

Pachycephalosaurus

Anatosaurus

Struthiomimus

Scolosaurus

Rutiodon

Psittacosaurus

It was morning. Albertosaurus stirred drowsily. He had spent the night in the warm, dark shelter of a clump of willows on the flood plain. He looked out at the great green expanse of cattails glistening with dew. The plain seemed still and silent.

Albertosaurus had killed and eaten early the day before. Full, heavy and content, Albertosaurus had spent the rest of that day sleeping. Now he was very hungry again.

The willows hid his enormous frame well. Close by ran a trail to a crescent-shaped lake used as a water hole by other animals. Albertosaurus had decided to lay in wait for them.

The sun rose slowly behind the long, thick, dark line of trees along the lake. Tiny biting insects buzzed around Albertosaurus and he shook his huge head irritably.

The movements disturbed a snake in the branches above him, and it slithered away. Albertosaurus waited impatiently. There were no signs of movement on the plain, but he watched a spider spinning a web among the rushes.

A little mammal jumped out of the undergrowth. Albertosaurus made a half-hearted lunge at it, but the creature turned and fled at the first sign of movement.

Albertosaurus settled back to watch the plain. He was bored, perhaps he would move on.

His gaze wandered over the plain. A gray shadow caught his attention. Suddenly alert and absolutely still, he watched as the gray patch grew larger and closer. Soon it was possible to make out a large herd of Triceratops. Albertosaurus could feel their great weight shaking the ground.

The herd closed in on his hiding place. Still he waited, his eyes searching for the weakest, most vulnerable animal. Then he saw it, a young female on the edge of the herd. Head down, and with a roar, Albertosaurus attacked. The shocked herd stopped and wheeled about to face Albertosaurus. His great teeth came down on the female's neck as she turned to defend herself. Her horns made contact with Albertosaurus, and tore at his thigh. Albertosaurus dropped back in pain.

The Triceratops stood, swaying slightly, blood dripping from her frill. Albertosaurus prepared to attack again, but a large male put himself between Albertosaurus and his quarry.

Other males had stationed themselves all around the edge of the herd. Albertosaurus was now faced with a defensive circle of heavily armored angry males. The male in front of him pawed the ground. Albertosaurus turned away. He had no wish to be charged at by an animal the same height as himself and much heavier. Roaring with frustration he retreated into the trees.

The herd moved on. Albertosaurus followed, hoping that the wounded Triceratops would fall behind and he could attack again.

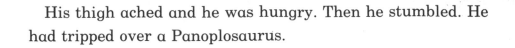

His thigh ached and he was hungry. Then he stumbled. He had tripped over a Panoplosaurus.

Albertosaurus looked down. The Panoplosaurus lay clutching the marshy ground in terror. Albertosaurus tried to turn it over with his huge hind legs. He kicked and scratched at it, but the Panoplosaurus held fast, frantically digging its feet further into the earth.

Albertosaurus' claws made no impact whatever on its armored back, and eventually, shaking his head with annoyance he gave up.

Albertosaurus decided to head back to the lake, hoping to find possible prey there. Birds flapped up from the rushes as he approached, and in the distance a lone Stegoceras saw Albertosaurus. The lone Stegoceras turned and fled.

The lake was quiet and peaceful. Dragonflies darted low over the lily pads, and soft-shelled turtles sunned themselves, occasionally dropping back into the water with a splash. Otherwise, the lake was deserted.

Albertosaurus turned toward the river in the hope of finding a meal there.

The forest was dark and cool after the bright sunlight of the plain. Birds, disturbed by his presence fluttered above him, and the occasional lizard darted in and out among the tree trunks.

Albertosaurus pushed his way through the saplings and ferns, toward the river bank.

Suddenly he stopped. Albertosaurus listened. Above the noise of the river his sharp hearing had picked up the bellow of a Hadrosaurid. Here was another chance for a kill.

Albertosaurus set off along the bank, keeping a line of dense, tall rushes between him and the river. He drew level with the noise and stopped again.

He moved forward cautiously until he could see a herd of Saurolophus on a sand bar. They stood chewing conifer needles, unaware of his presence. Albertosaurus studied the herd, chose an elderly female, and attacked.

The herd turned in terror as Albertosaurus' huge bulk thundered across the sand. Bellowing, they threw themselves into the river and swam for their lives.

The old female was too slow. Albertosaurus lunged at her neck, his huge mouth wide open. She sank down under the impact, her long tail lashing desperately in the shallows. Albertosaurus closed his powerful jaws, and she lay still.

Albertosaurus stood over her triumphant, then he began tearing at the carcass. A pair of crocodiles, drawn by the smell of blood, scavanged at the tail.

Albertosaurus ate his fill. Then, heavy and content, he walked back to the bank. In a hollow among the rushes and lilies and in the shade of some sycamore trees, Albertosaurus lay down and slept.

Quetzalcoatlus

Parasaurolophus

Deinosuchus

Corythosaurus

Oviraptor

Spinosaurus

38

Corythosaurus

Written by Frances Swann
Illustrated by Pam Mara

Pachycephalosaurus

Anatosaurus

Struthiomimus

Scolosaurus

Rutiodon

Psittacosaurus

Dusk was falling over the great oak forest as the Corythosaurus herd began to settle for the night. Gradually the familiar sounds of the day faded, and the warm air was filled with the rustling noises of the night.

A little way from the herd, a pair of
Stenonychosaurs hunted their evening meal of small
mammals. The Corythosaurs watched the
Stenonychosaurs lazily as they darted over the forest
floor, their large eyes missing nothing. Satisified, the
two Stenonychosaurs departed, and in the fading
light, Corythosaurus and her herd fell asleep.

Corythosaurus awoke to the familiar smells of the forest on a spring day. She felt hungry. The herd gradually gathered together and moved off. Walking slowly on all fours, they headed toward the river. Corythosaurus, the other females, and the youngsters stayed in the center of the herd. The males, ever watchful, surrounded them.

When they arrived at a cypress grove, the herd spread out to feed. Standing on her back legs, Corythosaurus reached up and broke off twigs with her jaws. As she chewed she watched last year's youngsters forage in the undergrowth. She felt content. The forest was peaceful. Over the last few weeks the sounds of the males' noisy mating displays had filled the air. Soon Corythosaurus would return to the nest site to lay her eggs in the sand.

Well fed, the herd regrouped and moved on. The undergrowth was thicker now. The canopy of poplar and willow leaves above them let in more light, and Corythosaurus could feel the sun on her back.

Suddenly aware of movement, the herd stopped and stared in astonishment. There before them was a pair of male Chasmosaurs. Both were nodding their great-frilled heads violently from side to side in a mating display. Then, apparently unaware of the herd's presence, they charged each other, locking their browhorns together.

The herd was startled into action by the noise and moved quickly away toward swampier ground.

The air was hot and humid, and the smell of rotting vegetation and stagnant water hung in the air. Corythosaurus nibbled from the china firs as she walked. Beneath her feet the wet ground was littered with fallen moss-covered branches. Every so often, a heron flapped lazily away as she approached.

A Struthiomimus appeared. Agile and alert, it ran backwards and forwards hunting the dragonflies that skimmed the pools. Corythosaurus watched it with curiosity. Soon it caught a frog with a loud snap, swallowed it, and ran off toward the forest.

A sudden commotion at the edge of the forest brought the herd to an abrupt halt. In the split second before she fled, Corythosaurus saw a lone Centrosaurus cornered by an Albertosaurus. Its huge frame towered over its prey. As the Centrosaurus charged, the Albertosaurus wavered and then turned away.

Terrified, Corythosaurus and her herd raced for the safety of the river. On reaching the water, they splashed out through the shallows until they could swim. Only when they knew the water was too deep for the Albertosaurus to reach them did they begin to relax.

The river was wide and winding. The herd swam upstream, keeping a careful distance between themselves and the shore. Corythosaurus felt exhausted. The sun reflected on the water and dazzled her eyes. Still the herd swam on. Above them Corythosaurus could see several Pteranodons, soaring on the warm air currents, probably heading for the sea.

The herd was now quite far away from
Albertosaurus. Corythosaurus felt safer and followed
the others into the shallows, where they waded quietly
in the warm water.

Rested, they moved back toward the swamp. A large herd of Parasaurolophus passed close by. The herds ignored one another, each knowing the other posed no threat.

Corythosaurus and the others fed as they skirted the edge of the forest. The light was fading slowly, and all seemed peaceful.

A strange distant noise stopped the herd. Corythosaurus stood alert. She scented the air, sensing danger. Suddenly over the heads of the leading males she could see the cause. On the other side of the swamp two huge Tyrannosaurs and an Albertosaurus were scavenging a dinosaur carcass. At their feet a pair of large crocodiles fought over the remains.

Intent on their meal, the Tyrannosaurs appeared not to have noticed the herd. Once again, the herd turned and fled. This time they ran headlong into the forest.

Only when they reached the protective darkness of the oak forest did they stop. Corythosaurus stood wearily, her flanks heaving. The herd would go no farther tonight. Corythosaurus found a soft part of the forest floor and lay down. Night was falling, and the day had been eventful. She was ready to sleep.

Quetzalcoatlus

Parasaurolophus

Deinosuchus

Corythosaurus

Spinosaurus

Oviraptor

58

Deinosuchus

Written by David White
Illustrated by Pam Mara

Pachycephalosaurus

Anatosaurus

Struthiomimus

Scolosaurus

Rutiodon

Psittacosaurus

It was still dark as Deinosuchus glided slowly through the river. He swam silently, his enormous bulk causing scarcely a ripple on the still water. Only the tip of his large snout and his small but ever watchful eyes could be seen above the surface.

Dawn was near. Growing light began to reveal the features of the riverside: muddy inlets, tall grasses and trees whose exposed roots seemed to writhe like snakes.

Deinosuchus had been active all night, snapping up fish and other small land creatures that had crossed his path. Now he was filled. In spite of his great size, he needed little food to sustain his life.

Deinosuchus needed to warm his blood. He swam toward the inlet that marked the boundary of his territory. With a mighty rush of water he surfaced. Plegadornis, hunting in the shallow waters of the inlet for frogs and water beetles, flew off in alarm. Lizards, alerted by the vast shadow of Deinosuchus, scurried into the long grass.

61

Deinosuchus drew his great length up the bank and lumbered toward the glade where he usually basked with his mate. Suddenly, he heard a long, drawn-out hiss. A few yards away, and across his path, stood another huge crocodilian. He was a rival of Deinosuchus, always ready to fight for the position of leader of the pack.

Deinosuchus did not hesitate. With a roar, he launched himself at his adversary. The riverbank seemed to shake with the shock of the impact. The two creatures twisted and turned, thrashing their huge tails. Each of them was trying to knock the other off balance. This would expose the throat and belly, the only areas of the heavily-armored creatures which were vulnerable to attack.

The struggle was soon over, for this was no fight to the death, but a trial of strength. Deinosuchus was clearly the stronger of the two. His rival accepted this and backed away. Hissing discontentedly, he slunk into the long grass and disappeared from view.

His dominance confirmed, Deinosuchus continued on his way. Soon he found the spot where his mate and other crocodilians were basking motionless in the sun. Deinosuchus settled his massive body on the grass and let the sun warm the cold blood in his veins.

By now the sun was rising in a clear blue sky. Butterflies and bees moved among the climbing roses and banks of saxifrage which surrounded the glade. As Deinosuchus basked, smaller creatures scampered by at a respectful distance. Struthiomimus appeared, plucking fruit and leaves from the trees with her long arms. Her appetite seemed insatiable, as she plucked insects from the air with her horny beak and grabbed at lizards in the long grass.

Deinosuchus remained watchful. Such creatures were poor prey, since they could easily outrun him. However, some of them could be a real threat. Velociraptor, in particular, had a taste for crocodilian eggs. Fortunately, the female crocodilians buried their nests very deep in the sand. By the time Velociraptor had discovered the eggs, Deinosuchus had usually discovered him. Velociraptor never stayed to argue, but darted off with astonishing speed.

When the sun had reached its highest point, and day was at its hottest, Deinosuchus stirred. By now his blood was warm. He felt active and alert. He raised his body from the ground and waddled across the glade. Now it was time to hunt in the cool shade of the forest pools.

A herd of Parasaurolophus were browsing on the upper branches of the pines at the forest's edge. Their teeth ground the tough needles to a green pulp. As Deinosuchus approached they moved away quickly, back to the trees which they had already stripped bare of foliage.

Deinosuchus entered the forest pool with surprising quietness. Even so the sound was enough to alert Alamosaurus, wading in the pool a hundred yards away. Alamosaurus slowly turned his head and gazed at Deinosuchus. Cautiously, he began to lumber away. Deinosuchus did not bother to follow, but slid down into the water, half in and half out, like a giant trunk of some fallen oak. Nearby, a python uncurled itself from a branch and disappeared into the ferns.

Deinosuchus had picked a good position. He was completely hidden by the shade of the forest. The sunlight which filtered through the pines and cypresses served only to camouflage him further. At the same time, he had a good view of the pool and of any creature who came to drink at it.

He did not have to wait long. A herd of
Corythosaurs moved slowly down to the waterside. Yards
from the pool, they stopped. Their keen sense of smell and
hearing warned them of danger. They could sense
Deinosuchus, although they could not see him.

One Corythosaurus, younger and more impatient
than the rest, walked down to the water and began to drink,
only inches from where Deinosuchus lay.

Deinosuchus took his chance. The water cascaded from his back as he rose from the pool. With one movement, he totally enclosed the head and shoulders of Corythosaurus in his gaping jaws. Corythosaurus struggled to get free, his feet kicking up sand on the riverbank. Alas, his struggles were in vain. Deinosuchus slowly, inexorably, drew the creature below the surface of the water. Soon the struggling ceased.

Deinosuchus was preparing to drag the dead Corythosaurus to his larder below the branches of a giant sequoia, when he heard a roar. The herd of Corythosaurs had vanished. In their place stood the towering figure of Tyrannosaurus.

Deinosuchus feared no creature, however large. He angrily turned to face Tyrannosaurus putting himself between him and the carcass of Corythosaurus.

Tyrannosaurus lurched forward, lunging at Deinosuchus in an effort to frighten him. Deinosuchus held his ground. Tyrannosaurus tried to snatch at the carcass. Deinosuchus lashed his tail fiercely, almost knocking Tyrannosaurus off balance.

Soon Tyrannosaurus grew tired. He wanted food not a fight. Eventually, he stalked away, leaving Deinosuchus with his prey. As Tyrannosaurus left, his body cast a giant shadow on the grass. The day was drawing to a close.

Rhamphorhynchus

Pteranodon

Pterodactyl

Ankylosaurus

Dimetrodon

Iguanodon

Tricondon

Nothosaurus

Written by Rupert Oliver
Illustrated by Roger Payne

Archaeopteryx

Ichthyosaurus

Plesiosaurus

Deinonychus

Nothosaurus

The storm was over. For days the wind had blown with tremendous fury and the huge waves had smashed themselves against the rocks, throwing spray into the air. Everything was quiet again now.

Nothosaurus had been frightened by the fury of the storm. She had taken shelter inland where the waves could not reach her. Now that the wind and waves had gone, Nothosaurus returned to the beach to look for food. She was very hungry, but she would be able to catch some fish out at sea. Carefully, Nothosaurus picked her way across the beach. The shoreline was scattered with the debris thrown up by the storm.

Using her powerful legs and strong tail, Nothosaurus swam out to sea. Nothosaurus was a strong swimmer, but something was wrong today. She could not swim as fast as usual. Inside her body Nothosaurus was carrying eggs. They were almost ready to be laid. It was the extra weight of the eggs that was slowing Nothosaurus down. Soon she would go ashore to lay her eggs, but now she was hungry.

In the air a pair of Rhamphorhyncus swooped and wheeled. Like Nothosaurus, the Rhamphorhyncus were hunting for fish. They could swoop down out of the sky and snap the fish up in their jaws. Nothosaurus noticed they were circling over one particular place. Slowly Nothosaurus swam over to where the Rhamphorhyncus were circling.

As Nothosaurus drew near to the
Rhamphorhyncus, she could see a school of fish
beneath the surface of the sea. Slowly, so as not to
frighten the fish, Nothosaurus swam nearer.
She judged the distance between herself and
the fish and when she was in the right position,
Nothosaurus dashed forward, but she had
forgotten that she could not move as fast as usual.
Before Nothosaurus could reach the school of fish, a
swift Mixosaurus had appeared. The Mixosaurus
dashed in among the school. It snapped up fish in its
sharp teeth and then swam on.

By the time Nothosaurus had reached the position of the school the fish had scattered in alarm Nothosaurus was still hungry but no matter how hard she tried, she was too slow to catch any fish. Perhaps the storm had washed some food up on to the beach.

Wearily, Nothosaurus swam back to the beach. She was feeling very hungry as she dragged herself out of the water. A sudden movement startled her. Another creature was on the beach.

Nothosaurus looked around carefully. The other creature might be a fierce hunter that would want to make a meal out of Nothosaurus. The creature was a Placodus.

Nothosaurus had nothing to fear. The Placodus and its companion walked past Nothosaurus and into the sea. There they splashed about, looking for shellfish on which to feed. Relieved that she was in no danger, Nothosaurus walked along the beach. She was looking for food.

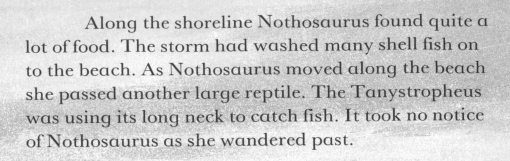

Along the shoreline Nothosaurus found quite a lot of food. The storm had washed many shell fish on to the beach. As Nothosaurus moved along the beach she passed another large reptile. The Tanystropheus was using its long neck to catch fish. It took no notice of Nothosaurus as she wandered past.

Having eaten enough food to last her for some time, Nothosaurus lay down to rest. She could not settle down. Something was troubling Nothosaurus. It was time for her to lay her eggs. Nothosaurus climbed to her feet and carried on walking.

Nothosaurus was looking for a place to lay her eggs. She knew that if she laid them out in the open, the eggs would soon be eaten by other creatures. She would have to hide them somewhere.

Before long, Nothosaurus came to the entrance of a cave. The cave would make a very good place to hide her eggs. The cave was close to the sea so that when the young Nothosaurs hatched out they would not have far to travel to reach the water. Few creatures lived in caves, so the eggs would not be found easily.

As Nothosaurus scrambled over the beach to reach the cave mouth she was startled by something passing over her head. The creature that glided past was a Kuehneosaur. Nothosaurus seldom saw a Kuehneosaur down on the beach. Kuehneosaurs preferred to live inland among the trees.

Nothosaurus walked into the cave.

The cave was damp and dark. As she entered the cave, Nothosaurus sniffed the air. There were no scents of other animals. Her eggs would be safe. As she peered into the dark, Nothosaurus could see that the cave was quite large and that moss grew on the walls.

Nothosaurus walked into the cave, slipping on some of the wet stones. Further in, the floor of the cave was dry and the air not so damp. This would be a good place to lay her eggs, thought Nothosaurus.

Using her forefeet Nothosaurus dug a shallow
hole. When she was satisfied with the hole
Nothosaurus stopped digging. Then she squatted
over the hole and began to lay her eggs. It took some
time, but finally she had laid all her eggs.

Nothosaurus began to cover the eggs with loose stones and sand. No sooner had she begun to do this than Nothosaurus heard a strange sound. Creaks and groans echoed around the dark cave. Then a stone crashed to the ground near to Nothosaurus. Looking up she saw a whole section of the cave roof give way and fall. The cave was collapsing.

The storm which had hit the shore had also weakened the cave walls. Once the first stone fell, it started a collapse. The rest of the cave was now falling in.

Nothosaurus stopped trying to cover the eggs. She ran for the cave mouth in a panic. All about her, boulders and rocks were smashing to the ground. If she did not escape soon, she would be buried alive beneath the stones. Nothosaurus raced for the daylight. A rock hit her a glancing blow but still she ran.

Gasping for breath Nothosaurus dashed out into the sunlight. Moments later the whole cave collapsed with a tremendous roar. Nothosaurus escaped. As soon as Nothosaurus realized that she was safe she lay down to rest. While she was lying exhausted a small furry Morganucodon scampered on to a rock.

Nothosaurus raised her head. The beach was peaceful and she was hungry. She would swim faster now. Nothosaurus splashed into the sea in search of fish.

Quetzalcoatlus

Parasaurolophus

Deinosuchus

Corythosaurus

Oviraptor

98 Spinosaurus

Parasaurolophus

Written by David White
Illustrated by Pam Mara

Pachycephalosaurus

Anatosaurus

Struthiomimus

Scolosaurus

Rutiodon

Psittacosaurus

Parasaurolophus woke as the first rays of the sun broke into the glade. The grass was heavy with dew and a mist hung over the lake. Around her, the herd was stirring. She could see their crests through the mist as they lifted their heads to sniff the morning air.

The strong scent of the sequoias drew them to their feet. They were hungry. Calmly, yet purposefully, they made their way to the edge of the pine forest and began to feed on the upper branches. Soon the woods were full of the sounds of their grunting as they chewed on the pine needles and called to each other through the trees.

Parasaurolophus did not go with them. Instead, she set off toward the lake. Near the water's edge she found what she was looking for: a long low mound of earth with an opening at one end. This was the nest that she had built for her young. She had made it by stripping the branches from a tree and covering them with mud.

A python lay curled on top of the nest. He was waiting patiently for the young to emerge. Parasaurolophus drove him away with a quick movement of her head. She pushed her snout into the entrance of the nest and snorted. Soon, the head of the first of her young appeared. He had to squeeze his body through the entrance, since he was now as large as many full grown dinosaurs.

Further along the lakeside, Parasaurolophus could see the crests of a herd of Corythosaurs that had come down from the forest to drink. Their young playfully splashed in the shallows. Suddenly, there was a roar and a rush of water. Deinosuchus launched himself at one of the Corythosaurs. For a moment, his mighty jaws could be seen as they gripped the neck of the animal. Then both disappeared into the reeds.

Parasaurolophus remained at the water's edge with her young. She knew that they were safe. Deinosuchus had found the food he needed and would not threaten them for a while.

When they had eaten enough, Parasaurolophus signaled to her young, with a series of grunts, that it was time to leave the lake. She then led them back to the nest. The sun was high in the sky. It was time for her to feed.

The danger past, Parasaurolophus swam back to the shore. She returned to the nest to see if all was well. She found the nest undisturbed and her young safe inside.

When the young ones heard Parasaurolophus arrive, they knew it was safe to leave the nest. Outside they fought mock battles while Parasaurolophus dozed in the heat of the afternoon. Struthiomimus sprinted by in her restless search for food. She paused near Parasaurolophus and parted the grass with eager hands. She was looking for lizards and insects.

Parasaurolophus knew she was no match for Deinonychus. All she could do was to act as a decoy, to draw Deinonychus away from the nest. Bravely, she ran toward him, snorting and grunting. Deinonychus paused in his digging and turned toward her. He seemed undecided as to what to do.

Parasaurolophus pretended to run away. This encouraged Deinonychus to give chase. Parasaurolophus desperately dodged this way and that in an attempt to escape. Deinonychus soon caught up with her. He slashed at her with his claw, opening up a great wound in her back.

Quetzalcoatlus

Parasaurolophus

Deinosuchus

Corythosaurus

Oviraptor

118 Spinosaurus

Struthiomimus

Written by Frances Swann
Illustrated by Pam Mara

Pachycephalosaurus

Anatosaurus

Struthiomimus

Scolosaurus

Rutiodon

Psittacosaurus

Struthiomimus moved away. He cut a path through
the thick ferns with a quick, trotting gait. Spiders' webs
sparkled with dew in the undergrowth, and birds fluttered
above him in the redwood trees.

Struthiomimus was hungry now. He began to search
among the giant leaves of the gunnera plants for beetles and
millipedes to eat. Then, bored with these, he chased
dragonflies. He darted back and forth, jaws snapping as he
caught them.

A sudden movement brought Struthiomimus to a halt.
A short distance away were two male Chasmosaurs. They
stood facing each other, swinging their heads violently from
side to side. Struthiomimus watched this display for a moment
then he turned and left.

No longer so hungry, Struthiomimus continued to explore. The closer he got to the flood plain, the thinner the forest became. Soon there were only clumps of trees in a great green expanse of cattails.

Struthiomimus moved faster now, alert and watchful. Pterosaurs circled over the plain, and he passed several Euoplocephalus peacefully eating cattail tubers. All seemed safe.

Struthiomimus ran fast, his tail held stiffly behind him. His speed quickly took him out of danger. Tired, he decided to rest next to a large lake.

A herd of Corythosaurs were drinking from the clear water. Struthiomimus joined them.

Refreshed, Struthiomimus began to relax. He searched out some young shoots, and stood chewing them. Everthing around him was peaceful. He watched the dragonflies darting low over the lily pads. At the bottom of the lake he could see a Champsosaur lying in wait for passing fish.

Struthiomimus had begun to hunt for soft-shelled turtles when it began raining heavily. He left the lake and headed for the cover of the trees by the river.

In the dry season the river was slow and sandy, but this was the wet season. The river was fast and deep.

Huge logs were being swept downstream, crashing together as they went. The noise was deafening. Struthiomimus pushed his way through thick ferns, keeping away from the bank. The canopy of redwood trees above him kept out the rain. Even so, the ground was wet and slippery.

Struthiomimus searched among the saplings for lizards to eat. He found only a large nest of ants, and a long-dead, half-eaten fish.

The rain had stopped now. In the hardwood forest all was still. Only the sound of the birds disturbed the silence. Struthiomimus remained watchful even so.

Tall yellow tulip trees, sweetgums, proteas and yellow ginkgo trees rose above him. In their shadow grew green, shiny figs, holly and laurel.

Many of the bushes were covered with creepers, wild grape, misteltoe and honeysuckle. They made an excellent hiding place for small mammals, and Struthiomimus hunted about for them greedily. Unsuccessful, he turned his attention to the forest floor. Here he was lucky to find a whole nest of little mammals. They made a good meal.

The light was fading, and dusk would soon fall over the forest. In the twilight, a pair of Stenonychosaurs darted back and forth across the fallen leaves. They watched Struthiomimus with their large eyes as he passed.

Struthiomimus found a soft, safe spot among the lilies and ferns and settled down. The warm evening air was filled with familiar smells and sounds. In a very short time Struthiomimus was peacefully asleep.

Megaceros

Saber Tooth Tiger

Cave Bear

Glyptodon

Written by Rupert Oliver
Illustrated by Bernard Long

Woolly Rhinoceros

Mastodon

Glyptodon

Rain had been falling for hours, ever since Glyptodon had awakened after her night's sleep. The beast moved hungrily through the downpour and plunged into a muddy hollow. Glyptodon lumbered across the muddy ground to the far side. As she climbed up and out of the hollow, rain ran down her back.

As she reached firmer ground, she suddenly halted in her tracks. A loud trumpeting sound blasted through the air. An Imperial Mammoth was tearing at the branches of a high tree. The Mammoth was helping itself to leaves that were far out of Glyptodon's reach.

A short distance away was a patch of fresh, green grass. Perhaps there would be plenty of new shoots for Glyptodon to eat among the young grass. Glyptodon wandered over and began to pick at the succulent shoots. As she grazed, Glyptodon realized that the rain was stopping. She looked up to the sky and grunted her satisfaction as warm sunlight bathed her back.

A giant Anteater ambled past Glyptodon as she ate. The Anteater walked across to a large termite nest and reared up on its hind legs. It used the powerful claws on its front legs to rip holes in the nest. As the termites streamed out to repair the damage, the giant Anteater licked them up with its long, sticky tongue.

A roar boomed across the land. Glyptodon looked around in surprise and alarm. It sounded as though a meat eater was nearby. A yellow and black jaguar leaped from the undergrowth. It roared again and sprang toward the giant Anteater, its sharp teeth and jaws ready to strike. The Anteater reared up onto its hind legs and slashed out with its powerful front legs. The jaguar caught a glancing blow from one of these claws and staggered back. It was not used to being hurt, and eyed the giant Anteater warily. Then, the jaguar attacked again. This time the flailing claws of the Anteater missed the big cat. The jaws of the jaguar struck home and closed around the giant Anteater's neck. The struggle was soon over and the jaguar settled down to his meal.

Although Glyptodon knew that once a hunter has eaten it is rarely dangerous, she did not like to be so close to a powerful killer. While the jaguar was busy tearing chunks of meat from the carcass of the giant Anteater, Glyptodon slunk away quietly.

As she left, a vulture fluttered down from the sky and came to rest near to the jaguar. It was soon joined by several others. When the jaguar was not paying attention, one of the vultures dashed forward and grasped a strip of meat in its beak then quickly retreated. When the jaguar had eaten its fill it left its kill and the vultures moved in. They squabbled and fought each other as they grasped for scraps of meat.

As Glyptodon walked ponderously around a bush, she came face to face with one of the most dangerous hunters she had ever encountered. In front of her stood a Saber Tooth Tiger. Glyptodon knew that she stood no chance at all of running away from the big cat. The Saber Tooth Tiger could run much faster than the heavy Glyptodon. Glyptodon realized that her only hope lay in her thick armor. Glyptodon crouched down and waited.

The Saber Tooth Tiger leaped at
Glyptodon, but soon found that his claws and teeth
could not pierce the heavy, bony armor of Glyptodon.
The big cat pawed curiously at the great beast and
snarled. Suddenly Glyptodon swung her massive tail
forward. The Saber Tooth Tiger had to leap
sideways to avoid being struck.

The Saber Tooth Tiger retreated a short
distance and then began to circle Glyptodon, looking
for a weak point in her armor. Glyptodon stayed
crouched on the ground since it was the only way in
which she felt safe. Glyptodon heard a rustling on the
far side of the bushes. The Saber Tooth Tiger
heard it too and stopped circling Glyptodon. Instead,
it crouched down and gazed in the direction of the
rustling.

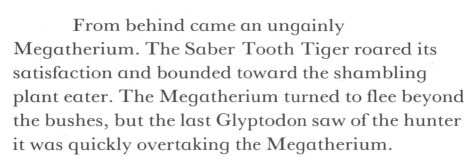

From behind came an ungainly Megatherium. The Saber Tooth Tiger roared its satisfaction and bounded toward the shambling plant eater. The Megatherium turned to flee beyond the bushes, but the last Glyptodon saw of the hunter it was quickly overtaking the Megatherium.

As soon as Glyptodon thought that she was safe from the Saber Tooth Tiger she stood on her feet. Glyptodon ambled off in search of more food. She spotted a large bush a short distance away which was heavy with fruit. She slowly moved toward it. She had not reached the bush when she realized something was wrong.

The ground beneath her feet was soft and sticky. With every step it became more difficult to lift her feet from the ground. Glyptodon started to become worried. Soon she found that she could not lift her feet at all. She was stuck firmly in the mud. Glyptodon howled her distress and struggled, but she could not work herself free. Soon a group of wolves were attracted by the noise and gazed hungrily at Glyptodon.

As Glyptodon struggled in the muddy ground she began to panic. Her limbs thrashed around and her feet slithered under her. The wolves sat and gazed at Glyptodon. They knew that if the large eater exhausted herself in the marsh she would make easy prey. Glyptodon might end up as a meal for the wolves.

Then, Glyptodon felt a patch of firm ground under one of her feet. Desperately, she tried to get a firm grip on the hard ground. First one foot, then another found a firm grip and Glyptodon hauled herself out of the marsh. Realizing that they were not going to find an easy meal, the wolves moved off.

Glyptodon lay panting by the sticky mud.
When she had recovered it was nearly evening. As
the sun began to sink below the horizon Glyptodon
plucked the berries from the bush. Before long, she
was joined by some bison who grazed on the long
grass which surrounded the bush. As darkness
spread across the landscape, Glyptodon lay down. It
had been an eventful day and Glyptodon was tired.

Megaceros

Saber Tooth Tiger

Cave Bear

Mastodon

Written by Rupert Oliver
Illustrated by Roger Payne

Woolly Rhinoceros

Mastodon

Glyptodon

Mastodon chewed happily. It had been a good Summer. The trees were full of juicy leaves. Mastodon had eaten plenty of food and now he had a comfortable layer of fat underneath his skin.

Now, however, the days were shorter and the weather was colder. Mastodon knew that Winter was coming. During the Winter, snow covered the ground, and food was scarce. The layer of fat which he had built up during the Summer would help to keep him warm and give him plenty of energy. Mastodon should be able to survive this Winter as he had survived so many others.

Mastodon moved off through the forest to find more food. As he walked through the trees a gust of wind struck Mastodon. The wind was chilly. Mastodon knew it would not be long until Winter came now.

Mastodon came to a small stream running through the forest. On the far side were some leafy branches which looked very tasty. Mastodon waded across the stream. Suddenly he stopped. There was something unusual about the stream. It was warm.

Mastodon liked the feel of warm water splashing around his feet. He stood in the stream for several minutes. Then he looked around to see where the stream was coming from. Perhaps there would be more warm water there. Mastodon could not see where the water was coming from so he decided to follow the stream.

After a short while, Mastodon found himself on the edge of the forest. In front of him stretched wide open countryside with hardly any trees on it. Pools of steaming water lay all around. Mastodon moved forward to stand in one of the pools. The water was comforting and warm. Suddenly a hole in the ground not far away gave out a rumbling sound. Then a great column of water shot up into the air. The geyser played to a great height for some time, then it stopped.

A loud trumpeting noise made Mastodon look around toward the forest. Some large animal was running through the trees. Then Mastodon heard the cries of wolves hunting. Mastodon turned to face the noise because wolves could be dangerous.

As Mastodon watched, a large Columbian Mammoth emerged from the forest. It stumbled on in fear into one of the pools of hot water. Mastodon could see that the Mammoth was lame. Wolves liked to hunt sick animals. The wolves bounded out of the forest and followed the Mammoth. Suddenly the ground underneath the animal gave way, and boiling mud gushed out. The Mammoth gave a cry of fright and then disappeared beneath the mud. A wolf also vanished in the mud. The other wolves ran back to the forest.

Mastodon was frightened. The Mammoth and the wolf had disappeared completely. The ground might give way under the feet of Mastodon. Mastodon lost no time in running away from the warm water. Having found dry ground again, Mastodon looked around.

All around him the plain rolled to the horizon. There was the occasional bush on the plain, but there were no trees from which to pluck leaves. Nearby some Pronghorns were grazing on the rich grass.

On the crest of a low, nearby hill were some bushes. Mastodon moved toward them to find out if their leaves tasted good or not. When Mastodon reached the top of the hill he stopped in surprise. He could see for miles, much further than he had ever been able to see in the forest.

Near the foot of the hill a small herd of horses grazed contentedly. Further away a vast herd of bison seemed to cover the entire plain. Mastodon did not feel safe in the open spaces. He wanted to return to his forest. Mastodon turned around and walked back down the slope.

Mastodon was careful not to walk across the pools of hot water. Instead, he walked around them and tried to find his way to the trees and firm ground. As Mastodon passed a large clump of bushes he heard something moving. A roar made Mastodon freeze in fear and an animal bounded into view. It was a Smilodon.

Mastodon knew that the Smilodon was one of the most dangerous hunters. Smilodon's long, sharp teeth made short work of any animal Smilodon attacked.

Mastodon stood facing the Smilodon. He lowered his head and shook his tusks at the big cat. Mastodon hoped that this would frighten the fierce Smilodon. The cat snarled at Mastodon, but did not attack. Smilodon seemed to be looking at something off to one side. Mastodon trumpeted loudly. The Smilodon turned and ran off towards a bison.

Mastodon watched until the Smilodon was out of sight. It chased the bison over a hill and Mastodon did not see if the bison escaped or not. When he was sure the Smilodon was gone and that he was safe, Mastodon moved off toward the forest.

Mastodon reached the trees, grabbed some leaves in his trunk and transferred them to his mouth. As Mastodon looked about him, a Glyptodon waddled past poking about in the undergrowth for some food. A fresh gust of wind blew a flurry of dead leaves around the feet of Mastodon. Winter was certainly arriving.

Megaceros

Saber Tooth Tiger

Cave Bear

Saber Tooth Tiger

Written by Rupert Oliver
Illustrated by Roger Payne

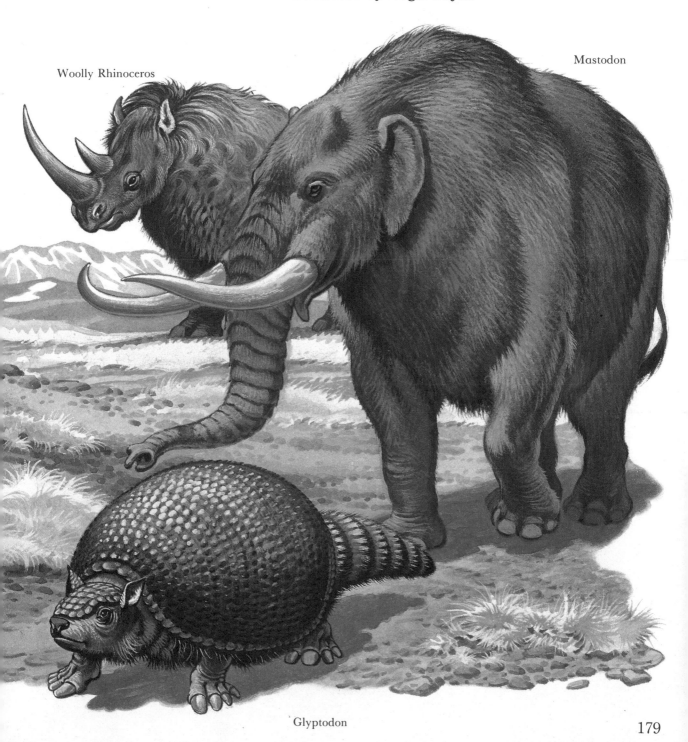

Mastodon

Woolly Rhinoceros

Glyptodon

The bushes rustled as a small bird leaped from branch to branch. It was Spring and the bird had to find a mate to help build a nest. Suddenly, the bird burst forth into song.

The chirping bird was making so much noise that he woke up a great, furry animal which had been sleeping under the bushes. As the large animal stirred and yawned, the bird stopped singing and watched.

The powerful Saber Tooth Tiger rose and smelled the air. He could smell blood and it was not very far away. He lifted his head and roared in satisfaction and the bird flew off in alarm. Saber Tooth moved off through the bushes, following the smell of blood.

As Saber Tooth emerged from the bushes he saw a strange sight. Just below him was a great pool of liquid, and in the pool was a group of snarling, fighting animals. In the middle of the pool was a great shaggy bison and all around it were hungry wolves.

The wolves were trying to kill the bison and had already wounded it several times. It was the blood from these wounds which Saber Tooth had smelled. Even though the bison had been injured, it was still fighting and was able to keep the wolves at bay. Saber Tooth remembered how good the taste of bison was and roared again. Then, he moved forward to join the wolves in the fight.

As Saber Tooth approached the pool of liquid he noticed something was wrong. The liquid was not splashing around like water. With all the fighting going on, there should be much spray. Then he noticed something else. All the animals in the pool were becoming stuck in a thick black liquid. Already the bison was beginning to sink into the pool and obviously could not get out.

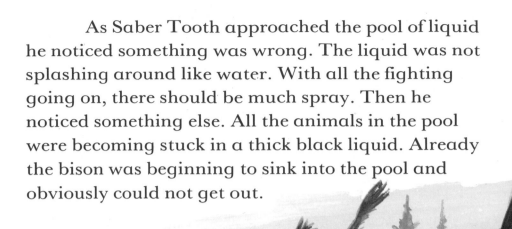

Perhaps if Saber Tooth joined in the fight he would also become stuck. Saber Tooth decided to leave the bison and wolves alone. He strolled off across the plain to look for something to drink. As he left, a vulture swooped down out of the sky. It had come to take any meat which the wolves might leave behind. Instead it, too, became trapped in the pool.

As Saber Tooth walked through the grass, he noticed a sudden flurry of movement. To his right was a herd of Pronghorns. The Pronghorns had been watching Saber Tooth in case he decided to attack them. They had not seen a Felis Trumani creeping up from the other side.

Suddenly, the Felis Trumani leaped from cover and began to chase the Pronghorns. Soon, it had singled out one Pronghorn which was slower than the rest. The Pronghorn bounded across the plain as quickly as it could, but Felis Trumani could run very fast indeed.

As the two animals raced past Saber Tooth, the Felis Trumani was catching up with the Pronghorn. Then, the Pronghorn put on a extra burst of speed and the Felis Trumani gave up.

Saber Tooth watched the Felis Trumani
standing exhausted. Saber Tooth could not run as
fast as Felis Trumani and had never been able to
catch a Pronghorn. He did not even bother trying to
attack the Pronghorn, instead he moved off toward
the river. Saber Tooth was thirsty so he hurried
toward the water. He followed a path down to the
river.

The path had fresh hoof marks, but Saber Tooth was more interested in water than food, so he did not attempt to move quickly. As he approached the water, a group of horses saw Saber Tooth. They neighed in alarm and galloped across the river to reach safety. Saber Tooth walked down to the river and drank his fill.

When Saber Tooth had finished drinking he realized that he had not had anything to eat since the previous day. He was very hungry. He moved away from the river and toward the grasslands. As Saber Tooth came over a rise in the land he saw a pile of meat lying on the ground. There was more than enough meat there for Saber Tooth. He walked toward the meat.

As he approached the meat, Saber Tooth suddenly halted in his tracks. Resting close to the meat were two of the only animals Saber Tooth feared. They were men. They were armed with spears which Saber Tooth knew to be dangerous. When the men saw Saber Tooth they started shouting and waving their spears. Saber Tooth snarled at them, then turning, he ran away. Even the savage Saber Tooth was frightened of man.

Saber Tooth was still hungry. He would have to go in search of living prey. Saber Tooth moved back toward the river. It was a very hot day and many animals would come down to the water to drink. Perhaps Saber Tooth would be able to catch one of them.

Saber Tooth moved down the path to the river until he came to a thick clump of bushes. Then, he moved off the path and hid himself in the bushes. From the bushes he would be able to spring out on anything which went past.

Saber Tooth settled down. He did not have to wait long. A group of horses moved down the path, but they smelled Saber Tooth and sped away for dear life.

It was a long time before another animal took the path toward the river. Then, Saber Tooth heard heavy footsteps. Something large was coming to drink. It did not run away so it could not have smelled Saber Tooth. Saber Tooth prepared to spring on the unwary newcomer.

Then, Saber Tooth saw what was coming. It was a huge Megatherium. As soon as the animal was close enough, Saber Tooth sprang out with a ferocious roar. The Megatherium heard the roar but before it could do anything to protect itself, the massive teeth of the huge cat were plunging deep into its back.

When Megatherium was dead, Saber Tooth began to eat. Saber Tooth ate as much of the fresh succulent meat as he could manage. Then, he walked off into the bushes to sleep.

Meanwhile, a pack of wolves moved in to finish picking the meat off the Megatherium. When Saber Tooth woke up there would be little left of his kill.

Megaceros

Saber Tooth Tiger

Cave Bear

Woolly Rhinoceros

Written by Rupert Oliver
Illustrated by Andrew Howat

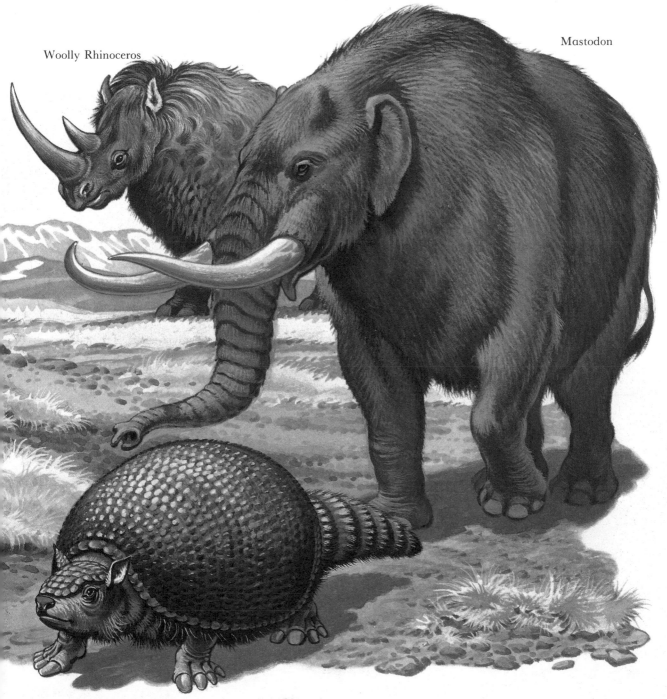

Mastodon

Woolly Rhinoceros

Glyptodon

Woolly Rhinoceros plodded through the patch of snow. Not far away was a piece of open land where the grass was beginning to grow. There would be some good food there. Close by, a small herd of Woolly Mammoths were feeding. They were sweeping their tusks to and fro in the snow, pushing it aside to reach the plants underneath.

In recent days the weather had been getting warmer. The snow, which had covered the whole land, had melted until only patches remained. Perhaps spring was coming and Woolly Rhinoceros would have to move North to avoid the hot weather which was so uncomfortable.

Suddenly, a group of men appeared, carrying sharp spears and axes. Woolly Rhinoceros knew that man could be very dangerous. Man was one of the most skilled hunters in the world.

The men did not seem to be very interested in Woolly Rhinoceros. They were paying more attention to the small herd of Woolly Mammoths. The Mammoths were slowly moving closer to the clump of bushes where the men were hiding.

One of the Woolly Mammoths moved close to the bushes. Suddenly a spear flew out from the bushes and buried itself in the side of the Mammoth. The animal roared in pain and turned to run away. Before it could move far, however, the men had sprung from cover and plunged even more spears and some axes into the creature. It was over in seconds and the Mammoth lay dead on the ground. Its roar had alerted the other Woolly Mammoths which quickly moved off. Woolly Rhinoceros, too, moved away from the men and their weapons.

Nearby was the sound of a splashing river. Spring must certainly be coming if the snow was melting. Woolly Rhinoceros walked down to the river to drink. As she approached the river bank Woolly Rhinoceros realized that she was not alone.

Peering intently into the waters was a Cave
Bear. Suddenly the claw of the Cave Bear lashed
down into the river and a fish flipped out on to the
bank. The Cave Bear had her young with her and
she allowed them to eat the fish. As the Woolly
Rhinoceros approached, the Cave Bear looked up.
She had nothing to fear from Woolly Rhinoceros, so
the Cave Bear went back to fishing.

Having drunk her fill, Woolly Rhinoceros climbed away from the river. On the open tundra the plants were starting to grow again after the long Winter. Grazing on the sparse grass was a large Megaceros. Close by was a small herd of Musk Oxen. Woolly Rhinoceros could smell the Musk Oxen before she could see them because they gave off a very powerful odor.

The Megaceros raised its head at a slight noise. Woolly Rhinoceros had heard it too and looked in the direction from which it came. Megaceros ran past Woolly Rhinoceros, calling out alarm. Woolly Rhinoceros could not see anything. Megaceros must have had better eyesight than Woolly Rhinoceros.

One of the Musk Oxen gave a cry of fear and the small herd began to bunch together. The young Musk Oxen stayed on the inside of the group while the adults stood around them. Across the tundra a pack of wolves came trotting. The adult Musk Oxen lowered their heads and presented their horns to the wolves.

The wolves did not even stop, nor did they try to attack the Musk Oxen. Instead, the wolves ran on across the plain, passing the plant eaters in peace. Perhaps they had smelled the blood of the Mammoth the men had killed. Wolves could usually pick up some scraps of food from such a kill.

The Musk Oxen spread out again into the loose formation. Woolly Rhinoceros started to graze on the meager plants which grew on the ground. There were some tasty, succulent shoots here, but most of the food was coarse growth from last year. It would be some time yet before there would be enough fresh food for Woolly Rhinoceros to eat. All through the Winter she had lived off the fat she had stored up the Summer before. Now almost all the fat had been used and Woolly Rhinoceros was very hungry indeed.

Far to the West ominous clouds were banking up. Woolly Rhinoceros was too busy eating to notice them or to realize what they meant.

As Woolly Rhinoceros grazed she gradually moved away from the Musk Oxen. Soon she was all alone on the open tundra. The dark clouds were even closer now and, at last, Woolly Rhinoceros noticed that they were there. She sniffed the air and felt that a change in the weather was on the way.

Then Woolly Rhinoceros smelled something else. She had smelled that particular odor once before and knew that it meant danger. Loping across the grass, passing between the bushes was a Homotherium. Woolly Rhinoceros knew how sharp the fangs of a Homotherium were. She lowered her head toward the cat. The Homotherium spotted Woolly Rhinoceros and moved forward to attack. Woolly Rhinoceros knew that her best chance was to attack as well. She charged forward with her horn pointing upwards, hoping to hit the Homotherium.

She missed, but her charge had frightened the Homotherium. Woolly Rhinoceros turned and faced the Homotherium. The cat was getting ready to pounce. Woolly Rhinoceros charged again. Once more the Homotherium had to get out of the way.

Woolly Rhinoceros was now getting tired. She could not charge many more times and when she stopped charging the Homotherium would be able to attack her. It was then that the dark clouds passed overhead and the last blizzard of the Winter struck. The wind whipped past the two animals and the snow fell down in a solid curtain. The Homotherium disappeared in the snow and Woolly Rhinoceros was able to escape in safety.

FACTS ABOUT DINOSAURS

The Skeleton of Albertosaurus compared in Size with a Man

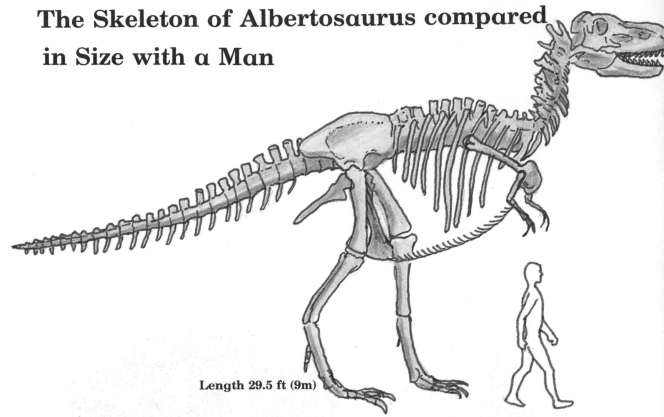

Length 29.5 ft (9m)

Albertosaurus and the Cretaceous World

The Age of the Dinasaurs

The word dinosaur is derived from two Greek words meaning "terrible lizard." All the dinosaurs lived in the Mesozoic era, 225 to 65 million years ago, at a time when the continents were much closer than today. At one time, much of the land was one giant continent called Pangaea. This great mass broke up over many millions of years, and segments drifted apart to become our present-day continents.

No man has ever seen a dinosaur – man did not appear on earth until a mere 2 to 3 million years ago. So how do we know so much about the dinosaurs?

Fossil Finds

Our knowledge comes from fossils which have been discovered all over the world. Fossil skeletons, eggs, nesting sites, tracks, dung, imprints of skin, and even mummified stomach contents have been found. New finds constantly update our view of the dinosaurs and their world.

When Albertosaurus lived

The Mesozic age is divided into three eras – the Triassic, Jurassic and Cretaceous. Albertosaurus lived at the end of the Cretaceous era, which lasted from 136 to 65 million years. The word Cretacious means "chalk." During this time great beds of chalk were formed, and the continents took on their present shapes. At the start of the Cretaceous era the weather was mild, but by the end it was much colder.

The land was low lying, and it was a time of high sea levels, with many deltas, rivers, lakes and swamps. Many new types of plants evolved during the Cretaceous period. Flowering plants appeared for the first time. By the end of the Cretaceous period many trees and plants had evolved which would be familiar to us today.

All about Albertosaurus

Albertosaurus was a tyrannosaurid dinosaur. The best known tyrannosaurid is Tyrannosaurus. Tyrannosaurus was 46 ft. long and weighed 7 tons. Albertosaurus was only 29.5 ft long and weighed 2 tons.

The tyrannosaurids were a fearsome family of meat eaters. They were powerfully built, with giant skulls, massive hind legs, and strong jaws. Their front legs were ridiculously small. These may have been useful during mating, or perhaps as a leverage when rising from the ground.

Albertosaurus was small and light for a tyrannosaurid. He would have ambushed his prey but been unable to chase it for any great distance. Large dinosaurs were too heavy to tackle, but the plentiful Hadrosaurids would have made easier prey.

Enormous jaws with rows of serrated teeth meant that Albertosaurus could slice through skin and meat, eating chunks of flesh and bone whole.

Fossils of Albertosaurus have been found in Alberta, Canada and Montana.

While Albertosaurus weighed 2 tons, Diplodocus (above) weighed about 26 tons.

Corythosaurus and the Cretaceous World

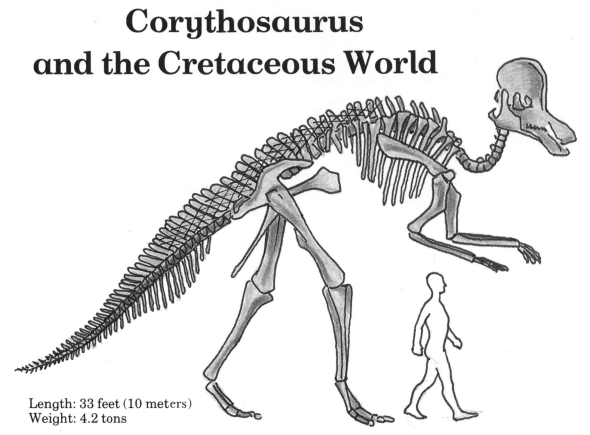

Length: 33 feet (10 meters)
Weight: 4.2 tons

The skeleton of Corythosaurus compared in size with a man.

The Age of the Dinosaurs

The word dinosaur is derived from two Greek words meaning ''terrible lizard.'' All the dinosaurs lived in the Mesozoic era, 225 to 65 million years ago, at a time when the continents were much closer to one another than they are today. At one time much of the land was one giant continent called Pangaea. This great land mass broke up over many millions of years, and segments drifted apart to become the continents as we know them today.

No human being has ever seen a dinosaur. Human beings did not appear on earth until 2 to 3 million years ago. How do we know so much about the dinosaurs?

Fossil finds

Our knowledge comes from fossils that have been discovered all over the world. Scientists have found fossil skeletons, eggs, nesting sites, tracks, dung, imprints of skin, and even mummified stomach contents. Every day new finds tell us more about the dinosaurs and their world.

When Corythosaurus Lived

The Mesozoic Age is divided into three eras: Triassic, Jurassic, and Cretaceous. Corythosaurus lived at the end of the Cretaceous era, which lasted from 135 to 64 million years ago. The word Cretaceous means chalk. During this time great beds of chalk were laid down, and the continents took on their current shapes. At the beginning of the Cretaceous era the weather was mild, but by the end it had become much colder.

The sea levels were high, and the land was low-lying, with many deltas, rivers, lakes and swamps. Many new kinds of plants evolved during the Cretaceous era. Flowering plants appeared for the first time. By the end of the Cretaceous period many trees and plants existed that would be familiar to us today .

All About Corythosaurus

Fossil remains of Corythosaurus have been found in South America, Asia, Europe, and North America. Corythosaurus was a Hadrosaurid dinosaur, often called a ''Duckbill.''

218

Corythosaurus was a medium-sized dinosaur who could walk on either two or four feet. Her paddle-like hands and strong, deep tail show that she could certainly swim. This ability to swim was her main defense against predators.

Corythosaurus had a sharp, horny, tortoise-like beak. Fossilized stomach remains show that Hadrosaurids fed on conifer needles, twigs, land plants and seeds. Corythosaurus had hundreds of large grinding teeth; some Hadrosaurids had over a thousand teeth.

The word Corythosaurus means "helmet lizard." A male Corythosaurus had a larger crest than the females and the young. It is thought that displaying males used their crests as a signal. They also signaled by making noises.

Corythosaurus would have laid eggs and probably used the same site each year to nest and care for her young.

Like Corythosaurus, Ornitholestes (above) fossil remains also were found in North America.

The reconstructed skeleton of Deinosuchus compared in size with a man.

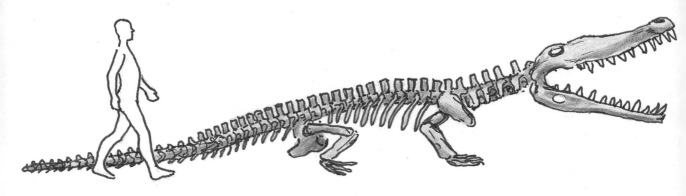

Length: Only a 6 ft (1.8 m) skull has been discovered. This would give Deinosuchus a probable length of 40–50 ft (12–15 m).

Deinosuchus and Late Cretaceous Texas

The time of Deinosuchus

Scientists divide the Earth's history over the last 600 million years into three eras – the Paleaozoic, Mesozoic and Cenozoic. They subdivide these eras into periods. The Mesozoic ("middle era"), known as the Age of the Dinosaurs, had three periods – the Triassic, Jurassic and Cretaceous. The Triassic period lasted from 225 to 195 million years ago, the Jurassic from 195 to 136 million years ago, and the Cretaceous – the longest period of all – from 136 to 65 million years ago. The Cretaceous period was the time of Deinosuchus.

The land of Deinosuchus

The fossilized remains of Deinosuchus have been found in the rock formations of the Rio Grande, Texas. The area is rich in dinosaur remains. Indeed, the entire range of known dinosaur orders and suborders of the Late Cretaceous period have been discovered in locations in western North America and Alberta, Canada. The land was changing fast at that time. The seas had flooded Europe and receded from North America, leaving behind inland seas and areas of swamp. Flora and

fauna which are familiar to us today were evolving. Trees like magnolia, plane and oak, flowering plants, moths, butterflies and pollinating bees, all began to appear. Giant sequoias and swamp cypresses grew in the swampy area where this story is set.

Family tree of Deinosuchus

Like dinosaurs, crocodiles evolved from the thecodont ("socket-toothed") reptiles more than 200 million years ago. The first Crocodilian was Protosuchus, whose remains were discovered in Arizona. This small, bony plated, amphibious reptile lived in the Upper (or later) Triassic period. In the Upper Jurassic and Lower Cretaceous a number of sea crocodiles known as Mesosuchians evolved. Earliest of these was Pelagosaurus, which fed mainly on fish. Sea crocodiles differed in many ways from land crocodiles. They had no armor plating and they had flippers instead of limbs. Mesosuchians were followed by land-based sebecosuchians, and amphibious Eusuchians—the only kind of crocodile that survives today. Deinosuchus was a Eusuchian.

Other meat-eaters

Many kinds of carnivorous (meat-eating) dinosaurs lived at the time of Deinosuchus. Perhaps the most impressive was Tyrannosaurus, the largest biped (two-footed) ever to walk the earth. Although we know what Tyrannosaurus and the other Carnosaurs looked like, we do not know how they lived. The traditional view is that these creatures were cold-blooded. If so, they would not have had the energy to pursue their prey. Instead they would have relied on ambush, or scavenged the remains of other animals' kills. However, some scientists now believe flesh eaters were warm blooded. If this was so, they may have hunted their prey, singly or in packs, over long distances. Coelurosaurs such as Struthiomimus and Velociraptor are always counted as flesh-eating dinosaurs but actually they were descendants of flesh-eaters who had become mainly vegetarian. They should perhaps be described as omnivorous, because they ate anything they could find—including dinosaur eggs.

Plant eaters

Herbivores (plant-eating animals) far outnumbered carnivores in this period. There were still a few giant Sauropods, such as Alamosaurus (named after the Alamo in Texas). However, most of the famous Sauropods, such as Diplodocus, had died out million of years before. Their place was taken by Ornithopods, notably the Hadrosaurs, such as the helmeted Corythosaurus and the tube-crested Parasaurolophus. (Nobody knows the purpose of these crests. They may have been recognition signals). These creatures, which are also known as duck–billed dinosaurs, were immensely successful, spreading from Asia to Europe and North America. The secret of their success may have been their teeth, which could grind down the toughest foliage for food. Had the Carnosaurs not kept their numbers down, they would have browsed the forests bare.

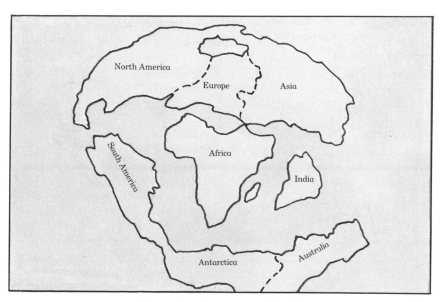

Map of the Cretaceous World

Nothosaurus and Triassic Europe

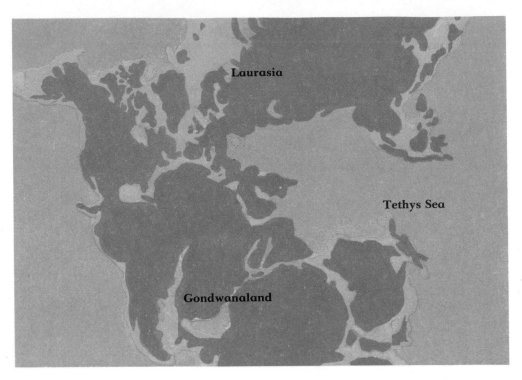

A map of the world during late Triassic times. Nothosaurus lived around the shores of the Tethys Sea. The outlines of modern continents are shown in dark brown.

When did Nothosaurus live?

Nothosaurus roamed the seashore about 210 million years ago. It lived during the Triassic period which lasted from 225 million years ago until 195 million years ago. The Triassic was the first period in the Age of the Dinosaurs, which is known as the Mesozoic Era. The other two periods in the Mesozoic were the Jurassic and the Cretaceous. The Mesozoic Era ended 65 million years ago.

Where did Nothosaurus live?

In the days of the Nothosaurus the continents of the world were very different from those of today. For instance, north-east Africa and India were not then joined to Asia. Instead, there was a large ocean which stretched from Spain right across to Australia and south-east Asia. Scientists have named this ancient ocean Tethys.

It was on the shores of Tethys that the Nothosaurus lived and hunted. In the middle of the Tethys, where Poland is today, was a large island which scientists have called the Isle of Gliny. The rocks of this island have produced some very important fossils. From these fossils scientists have learned much about the animals that lived there. It is on the rocky shores of the Isle of Gliny that our story is set.

What did Nothosaurus eat?

Because there are no Nothosaurs alive today, we cannot say for certain what they ate. Scientists have to collect fossil evidence and then decide what these large reptiles were most likely to have eaten when they were alive.

We know that Nothosaurus lived on the seashore so it must have found its food there. By studying the bones of Nothosaurs, scientists have found that they were very good swimmers and probably spent much of the time in the sea. A hunter will spend most of its time where there is plenty of food. Therefore Nothosaurus must have found most of its food actually in the sea. The fossilized teeth of Nothosaurus are sharp and pointed. These would have made the animal's jaws into a fish-trap. Nothosaurus ate fish.

Young Nothosaurs

Nothosaurus was a reptile and this meant that it laid eggs. Reptiles cannot lay eggs in the water so Nothosaurus had to come ashore to lay its eggs. It is thought that the mother Nothosaurus would abandon her eggs soon after she laid them. The young Nothosaurs would have to look after themselves. Many fossils of young Nothosaurs have been found in what were once caves. Perhaps caves were safe places to hide. As soon as a young Nothosaurus was old enough, it would leave the beach and head out to sea.

The Nothosaurus Family Tree

Nothosaurus was a reptile which lived about 210 million years ago. It must therefore have evolved from earlier reptiles. These reptiles probably lived on the land and were not very good swimmers. Unfortunately no one has found fossils of a reptile that could possibly be the ancestor of Nothosaurus. Therefore, we do not know how Nothosaurus evolved nor to which reptiles it is related.

Soon after Nothosaurus disappeared a new group of marine reptiles appeared; the Plesiosaurs. By studying their fossils, scientists have shown that the Plesiosaurs could have descended from Nothosaurus. The Plesiosaurus's neck was slightly longer than that of the Nothosaurus, and its head slightly smaller. Instead of the sturdy legs of the Nothosaurus, the Plesiosaurs had strong flippers, which were much better for swimming. Apart from these differences the skeletons of the Plesiosaurs were very like those of the Nothosaurs. This is why scientists think that they may be related.

Other Triassic Reptiles

Nothosaurus encounters several other reptiles that where alive during the Triassic period around the shores of Tethys. Perhaps the most unusual of these reptiles was **Tanystropheus.** The long neck of this reptile was inflexible. Tanystropheus could not move its head around very easily. The Rhamphorhynchus were among the first Pterosaurs to take to the air. Perhaps the most unusual was Keuhneosaur. The wings of this animal were, in fact, extended ribs. Though a fossil of this animal has been found near Tethys, it was much more common inland to the northwest. Placodus was a strange marine reptile that probably ate shellfish.

A Plesiosaurus

After millions of years the Nothosaurus line probably evolved into the Plesiosaurus, which first appeared during the Jurassic period.

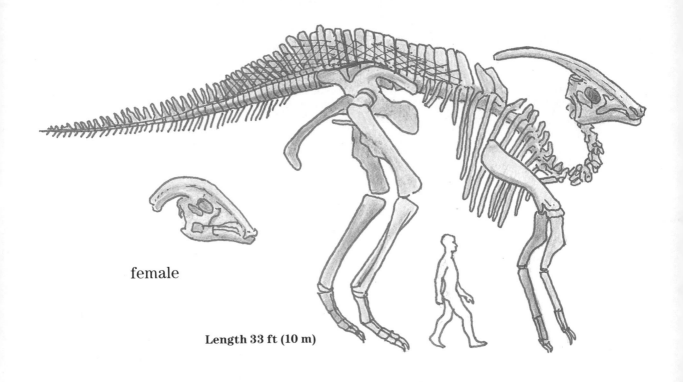

female

Length 33 ft (10 m)

The skeleton of Parasaurolophus compared in size with a man.

Parasaurolophus and Late Cretaceous Montana

The Time of Parasaurolophus

Geologists divide the Mesozoic Era, the "age of the dinosaurs," into three periods: the Triassic, the Jurassic and the Cretaceous. The Triassic lasted from 225 million to 195 million years ago, the Jurassic from 195 million to 136 million years ago and the Cretaceous—the longest period of them all—from 136 to 65 million years ago. This period was named after the great beds of chalk which were laid down at the time ("creta" is Latin for "chalk"). Parasaurolophus lived in the latter part of the Cretaceous, often known as the Upper Cretaceous, some 80 million years ago.

The Land of Parasaurolophus

In the Late Cretaceous, the continents started to take the shape they have today. While seas flooded Europe, they receded from North and South America, which became joined for the first time. The land was much flatter than it is today, with a vast inland sea extending from the Gulf of Florida to the Hudson Bay. The great mountain chains of the Rockies and the Andes had not yet been thrust up by movements of the earth's crust. However, much of the landscape would be familiar to us today, with many trees, flowers and birds that we would recognize. The story takes place in what is now Montana, an area which was thickly populated with dinosaurs. We know this because the fossilized remains of every order and suborder have been found in the sandstone rocks.

The Family Tree of Parasaurolophus

Parasaurolophus was a Hadrosaur, or duck-billed dinosaur. Hadrosaurs were probably the most successful of all dinosaurs. They were descended from the bird-hipped Camptosaurus. The earliest Hadrosaur, Bactractosaurus, lived in Mongolia in the early Cretaceous period. By the end of the Cretaceous, Hadrosaurs were established in Europe and Asia. The greatest number, however, were found in North America, where they evolved into many different types. Three main groups developed: the flat-headed, the solid-crested and the hollow-crested. Parasaurolophus, perhaps the most remarkable looking of all, belonged to the hollow-crested group. There have been many arguments about the purpose of these strange crests. Scientists think that the extended nasal passages inside the crests may have given them an acute sense of smell—enabling them to sense danger and increasing their awareness of each other.

Other plant-eaters

Herbivores far outnumbered carnivores in this period. The enormous lumbering Sauropods still wallowed in the swamps. Ornithopods (bird hipped) became more numerous and varied. There were three main groups of plant-eaters in the Late Cretaceous: the Hadrosaurs, the Ankylosaurs (the armored dinosaurs) and the Ceratopsians (the horned or frilled dinosaurs). Triceratops, was one of the most successful Ceratopsians and survived in large numbers right to the end of the Cretaceous.

Meat-eaters

In the Cretaceous period, the plant-eaters fed on the forests and the flesh-eaters fed on the plant–eaters. Carnivorous dinosaurs had an important function keeping the numbers of plant-eaters down and preventing the over-grazing of the forests. The late Cretaceous was the heyday of the carnivorous dinosaurs. There were two types: the mighty Archosaurs and the generally smaller but faster Coelurosaurs. Tyrannosaurus and Gorgosaurus were notable examples of Archosaurs, while Deinonychus and Struthiomimus were very different examples of Coelurosaurs.

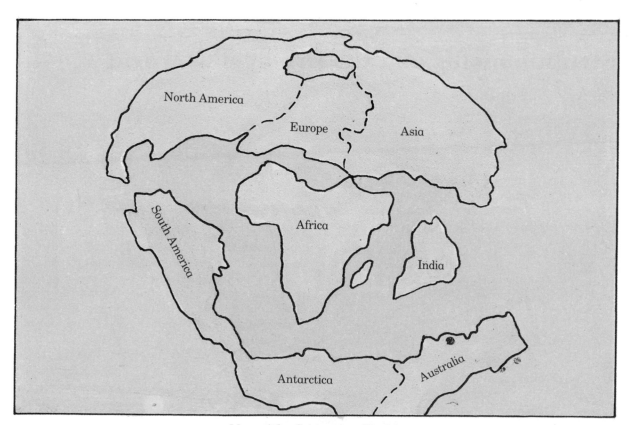

Map of the Cretaceous World

The Skeleton of Struthiomimus

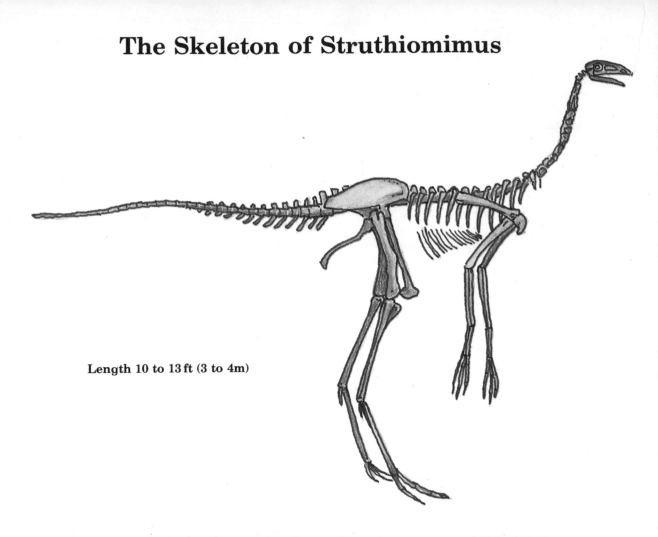

Length 10 to 13 ft (3 to 4m)

Struthiomimus and the Cretaceous World

The Age of the Dinosaurs

The word dinosaur is derived from two Greek words meaning "terrible lizard". All the dinosaurs lived in the Mesozoic Era, 225 to 65 million years ago, at a time when the continents were much closer than today. At one time much of the land was one giant continent called Pangaea. This great mass broke up over many millions of years, and segments drifted apart to become our present day continents.

No man has ever seen a dinosaur—man did not appear on earth until a mere 2 to 3 million years ago. So how do we know so much about the dinosaurs?

Fossil Finds

Our knowledge comes from fossils which have been discovered all over the world. Fossil skeletons, eggs, nesting sites, tracks, dung, imprints of skin, and even mummified stomach contents have been found.

New finds constantly update our view of the dinosaurs and their world.

When Struthiomimus lived

The Mesozoic Era is divided into three periods—the Triassic, Jurassic and Cretaceous. Struthiomimus lived at the end of the Cretaceous period, which lasted from 136 to 65 million years. The word Cretaceous means chalk; during this time great beds of chalk were formed, and the continents took on their present shapes. At the start of the Cretaceous period the weather was mild, but by the end it was quite a lot colder.

The land was low-lying, and it was a time of high sea levels, with many deltas, rivers, lakes and swamps. Many new types of plants evolved during the Cretaceous period. Flowering plants appeared for the first time. Many of these plants would be familiar to us today.

Dinosaur Provincial Park

Fossil remains of all the animals mentioned in this book have been found along the Red Deer River in Alberta, Canada. This area is now known as Dinosaur Provincial Park.

Fossil bones, shells, wood, pollen, and leaf imprints have been found. These tell us which animals and plants lived there, and what the weather was like.

Scientists can also tell that the plains were often flooded, that the rivers were high in the wet season, and that, in the dry season, fires occurred regularly.

All about Struthiomimus

Fossil remains of Struthiomimus have been found in North America. They show that he lived between 75 and 70 million years ago Struthiomimus was a medium-sized Ornithomimosaur, or "ostrich dinosaur." These dinosaurs had many anatomical similarities to present day ostriches, and could probably run as fast. Struthiomimus had a small head on a long, mobile neck. He had no teeth, but probably a long, horny beak. The upper and lower jaw moved independently, so that food could be ground in the same way as a modern-day parrot eats.

Struthiomimus was capable of great speed. The chest, back, and lower tail were stiff. When running, the tail would be held out stiffly to counterbalance the animal's weight. Speed would have been Struthiomimus' only defense against predators. The front legs were short and slender, with three clawed fingers. The back legs were very long, with three claws similar to those of present-day running birds. Struthiomimus' diet was probably omniverous that is, it ate both plants and animals. All the plants, insects and animals mentioned were contemporary with Struthiomimus, so it would have been a varied diet.

Stegoceras (above) also was found in North America.

FACTS ABOUT ICE AGE CREATURES

Glyptodon and Pleistocene America

Skeleton of Glyptodon

Heavy bones

Bony armor covering body
Height: 5 feet
Length: 8 feet

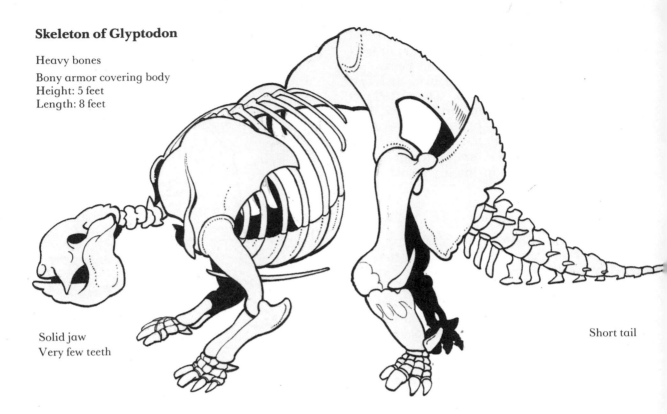

Solid jaw
Very few teeth

Short tail

The Age of the Glyptodon

Life has existed on Earth for many hundreds of millions of years. Scientists have divided this immense stretch of time into three great periods. The Palaeozoic, which means ancient life, lasted until 225 million years ago. During this era, invertebrates, fish and amphibians were the most important animals. During the Mesozoic Era, or age of middle life, reptiles were dominant on land, and these included the mighty dinosaurs. After the close of the Mesozoic, some 65 million years ago, the mammals became the most important form of life on earth. Mankind is a mammal and so are most of the larger animals alive today. The Glyptodon lived during the most recent period of the most recent era; the Pleistocene Period of the Holocene Era. During the Pleistocene Period, the Earth experienced some drastic changes in climate. For thousands of years the world was plunged into much colder weather and vast sheets of ice crept across the land. Then warm weather enveloped much of the earth in temperatures much hotter than usual. Such fluctuations occurred several times during the past 2 million years. Since

Glyptodon lived about 800,000 years ago, she experienced the Ice Ages, but she lived in Middle America where the temperatures were not so cold.

Glyptodon's America

Glyptodon lived in a period of time which was very important for the wildlife of North and South America. For millions upon millions of years, South America had been separated from all the other continents by a sea. North America, by contrast had been in touch with the other lands, and so had acquired a wide and varied wildlife. That of South America was generally highly developed, but had important flaws. Many groups of mammals which lived throughout the rest of the world did not live in South America and some South American mammals were rather primitive. When the two Americas came into contact with each other the two sets of mammals could cross the isthmus of Central America and compete for food. Glyptodon lived during the period of time in which the two Americas were sharing their wildlife.

Animals of the Two Americas

By the time the two Americas joined together, South America had been isolated for some 60 million years. Many strange and unique animals evolved in that period of time. All the meat-eaters on the continent were marsupials; that is, they carried their young in pouches like modern kangaroos. These animals were unable to compete with hunters which gave birth to live young. Within a very short period of time, all the South American hunters were extinct. They were replaced by animals from the north, such as wolves, jaguars, and Saber Tooth Tigers. Also, the plant-eaters of South America were very different. There was even a camel-like animal with a trunk. Most of these died out. However, a few managed to survive and some even moved into North America. Megatherium, the Giant Anteater, and Glyptodon itself were all South American animals. On the whole however, northern plant-eaters were more successful, and animals such as the bison and the Imperial Mammoth soon became the most numerous. The armadillo and tree sloth are South American animals that survive to this day.

Extinctions

By the time of Glyptodon, the two fauna of the Americas were mixing and settling down. Soon another animal appeared which totally upset the balance: man. Man arrived from Asia thousands of years ago and had a dramatic effect on wild animals by hunting them and by taking away their habitats. The ending of the last Ice Age, some 20,000 years ago, had just as great an effect. The two combined to cause the extinction of many American animals which had thrived alongside Glyptodon. Glyptodon itself soon became extinct and only its small relatives, the armadillos, survive. Also Megatherium has vanished leaving behind the sluggish sloths as its only relatives. The Imperial Mammoth has not only become extinct but it has left no living relatives. It has not been extinct for very long. Tales told to early explorers in South America by the local Indians suggest that Imperial Mammoths were still alive just 1,500 years ago. Among the hunters, the Saber Tooth Tiger died out around the end of the last ice age. It left behind the various cats of the two continents, though they are only distantly related. Other animals are still alive and some became incredibly successful. The Giant Anteater still tears at termite nests, and wolves and jaguars still hunt plant eaters. Perhaps the most successful of all was the bison. Within a short time after arriving on the North American plains from Asia, they took over. The native pronghorns were pushed to the edge of extinction. Millions of bison spread across the plains, grazing on the grass and being hunted by other animals, including man. At the start of last century, some 60 million bison roamed North America, one of the great success stories of the animal world. The bison, however, almost followed Glyptodon into extinction when men came to the plains. Today only a few thousand survive in special reserves.

The armadillo, modern relative of the Glyptodon.

Mastodon and the Ice Ages in America

The American Mastodon

Thick, hairy coat

Height: 10 feet
Length: 15 feet

Long, curved tusks

Sensitive trunk

Strong, pillar-like legs

The Pleistocene

The planet on which we live is very old indeed. It is about 4,600 million years old, though the oldest rocks which scientists have yet found are only about 4,000 million years old. Scientists have divided this immense period of time into four great eras. These are the Pre-Cambrian which lasted from the beginning of the world until about 570 million years ago. Only simple algae and other simple living things existed in this era. Next was the Palaeozoic Era, which means Ancient Life. This finished about 225 million years ago and fish and amphibians were the most important animals. The Mesozoic Era, which means Middle Life, was the third period of time. Reptiles, including the dinosaurs, were very important during the Mesozoic. The fourth and last era is the Cainozoic, which means Recent Life. Mammals have been the most important animals during the Cainozoic, which began 65 million years ago. The last period of the Cainozoic was the Pleistocene Period which began about 2 million years ago and only ended some 10,000 years ago. Our story is set during the Pleistocene Period of the Cainozoic Era.

Ice Ages

The climate of the world has not always been the same. During the Pleistocene the climate had varied widely and several Ice Ages had occurred. An Ice Age happens when the climate of the whole world gets very cold. In lands near to the North and South Poles snow falls, but does not melt. It keeps falling until it forms great sheets of ice many hundreds of feet thick. These sheets of ice reach out from the poles and cover great areas of land. Ice sheets also form in mountain ranges throughout the world. Even where there are no ice sheets, the weather becomes much colder than normal. During the coldest Ice Age of all, the polar ice sheets reached down from the North Pole to cover the whole of Canada and much of northern Europe and northern Asia. In between these periods of very cold weather, which lasted for thousands of years at a time, were periods of warm weather called Interglacials. During the Interglacials the climate was even warmer than it is today. Our story is set in North America, near the state of Tennessee, about 80,000 years ago. At this time a warm Interglacial was coming to an end and the last Ice Age was beginning.

The Mastodon

The Mastodon in our story is known to scientists as Mastodon Americanus. It was the very last type of Mastodon ever to live on earth. The Mastodons were a family of elephants which emerged about 25 million years ago and were very successful, evolving into a number of different forms. Mastodon Americanus first evolved some 300,000 years ago and only became extinct

230

10,000 years ago, when the American Indians were already on the continent. From the bones of this Mastodon, scientists can recreate its lifestyle. It would seem that the Mastodon lived in the thick woodlands that then covered so much of North America and it fed on the trees and bushes. The long, hairy coat which covered the Mastodon helped it to live through the severe winters which have always been a feature of North America. It also helped the Mastodon to survive the Ice Ages.

Ice Age Animals of North America

Eighty thousand years ago the wildlife of North America was different from that of today. There were, of course, some animals which can still be found today. The squirrels, bison and wolves in our story were common wild animals until Europeans travelled across America in the last century. Other animals in our story became extinct thousands of years ago and cannot be found today. The Mastodon itself, is long extinct. It died out at the end of the last Ice Age, about 10,000 years ago. The other elephant in our story, the Columbian Mammoth, died out somewhat earlier. It became extinct about 40,000 years ago. In its heyday, however, it had been a common animal on the open grasslands. It is possible that its place on the plains was taken over by the bison.

Bison had reached America by the time of our story. By the time man first came to America, bison roamed the grasslands in millions. It was not until the last century that they lost their dominance. The horse, which is today a common sight in rural America, is an unusual example. The American Horse, which appears in our story, was extinct by the end of the last Ice Age. By the time America was discovered by Columbus there were no horses in America at all. Every single horse to be seen today is descended from European horses, not the native American variety. The large Glyptodon was a 10 foot long relative of the modern armadillo. The large cat called Smilodon was the climax of many millions of years of evolution. About 30 million years ago the cat family split into two branches. These were the biting cats, which include all cats alive today, and the stabbing cats. Stabbing cats evolved long canines and powerful muscles which were capable of bringing down even the largest prey. Smilodon was one of the largest and most powerful of the stabbing cats, but it died out at the end of the last Ice Age.

Two curious members of the elephant family which are now extinct

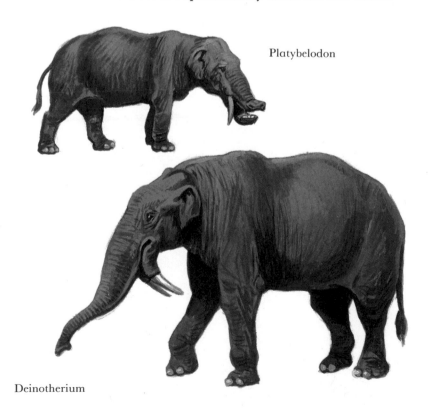

Platybelodon

Deinotherium

231

Saber Tooth Cats and their times

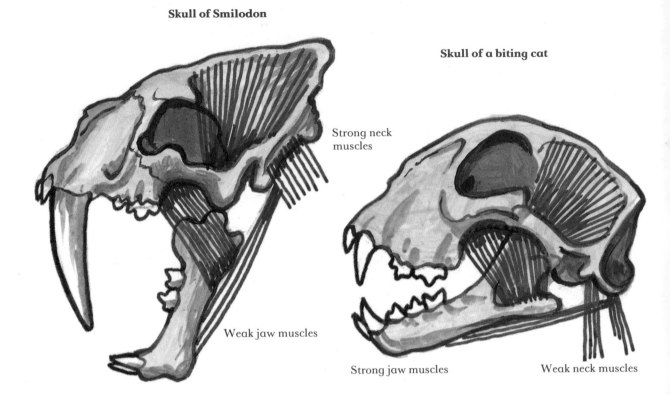

Skull of Smilodon

Skull of a biting cat

Strong neck muscles

Weak jaw muscles

Strong jaw muscles

Weak neck muscles

When did the Saber Tooth live?

There were many different species of Saber Tooth cats which lived at many different times. The earliest Saber Tooth cats lived about 30 million years ago and they lived all over the world, except in Australia. The Saber Tooth cat in the story is known today as Smilodon. Smilodon lived during the Pleistocene era, that is during the past two million years. There are no Saber Tooth cats alive today since they all died out about 11,000 years ago.

The Saber Tooth

Cats first appeared about 35 million years ago and almost from the start they divided into two lines. One was that of the biting cats. All cats alive today, including lions and tigers, belong to this group. The other group were the stabbing cats. Smilodon and all Saber Tooth cats were stabbing cats. Stabbing cats could not run as fast as biting cats and so hunted slower prey. In the story you can see the Felix Trumani running faster than Smilodon. In order to hunt large,

slow-moving prey, the stabbing cats evolved their massive canine teeth which have given them the name of Saber Tooth cats. Biting cats kill their prey by biting, but large prey cannot be killed so easily. The Smilodon therefore used its saber teeth to rip into prey. It is probable that Smilodon would plunge its fearsome teeth into its prey's neck and then use its powerful neck muscles to sever arteries and other blood vessels. Smilodon would then release its death-grip and wait for its prey to die from loss of blood. Since Smilodon died out some 11,000 years ago no cat has had such large teeth nor such powerful neck muscles.

Where did Smilodon live?

Smilodon lived in many parts of the world and was a very successful hunter. It even manged to reach South America, a land never reached by any cat before. The Smilodon in our story lived in North America, in what is now known as the state of California.

What were the tar pits?

The strange pools of liquid which the Smilodon came across early in our story were actually tar pits. Tar pits occur when oil seeps up from deep underground and collects in hollows on the surface. Any rain which falls onto a tar pit collects in pools on the tar's surface. Any animal passing which is thirsty is more than likely to attempt to drink this water. As soon as it steps onto the tar it is doomed. The weight of the animal drags it down into the sticky tar and it is unable to escape.

The tar pits of California turned to solid tar many years ago. In the tar were preserved the bones of all the animals which became trapped in the tar. Scientists have now dug up the tar and recovered the bones from the tar. Tar pits are therefore very important to scientists who study extinct animals.

There is one curious fact about the bones in the tar pits, and that is that there are far more meat-eaters, carnivors, than plant-eaters, herbivores. In reality there were far more plant-eaters than meat-eaters in California at the time. This anomaly can be explained by looking at what may have happened when an animal became trapped. A large animal such as a bison or mammoth would soon attract carnivores such as wolves or large cats. Any carnivore which stepped into the tar to attack the trapped animal would become trapped itself. It is for this reason that so many meat eaters have been found in the tar.

Other animals

Our story is set some 30,000 years ago. Though this is a long time to humans, it is only a short period in the history of the world. Many of the animals in our story can be seen today. The bison and Pronghorn are still to be found, as are the snakes, insects and birds of the time. Other animals have died out and are strange to us. One of these is the Megatherium. This beast was related to the tree sloths which survive today. In fact, it is often referred to as the giant ground sloth. It moved slowly and awkwardly and ate leaves from the trees. Some Megatheriums may have been as much as 18 feet long. Dire wolves have also become extinct, as has the Imperial Mammoth, an animal most people do not expect to see in America. The Imperial Mammoth, grew to be about 12 feet tall and had huge curving tusks which could measure a staggering 13 feet in length. Though the elephant is not usually associated with America, it is thought to have survived in South America until just a thousand years ago.

Dinictis. This ancestor of both stabbing and biting cats lived about 35 million years ago.

233

The Woolly Rhinoceros and the Pleistocene Ice Ages

Pleistocene Europe, showing the maximum extent of the ice sheets

The time of ice and snow

Life has existed on this planet for hundreds of millions of years, but it is only during the past 65 million years that mammals have been important. Scientists have named this era the Cenozoic, which means recent life, and have divided it into a number of periods. The most recent of these periods is known as the Pleistocene which began two million years ago. During the course of the Pleistocene the climate of the world had undergone sudden and dramatic changes. Before that time the climate of the earth remained fairly constant over millions of years. But during the Pleistocene it suddenly became much colder. Great rivers of ice, called glaciers, crept down the mountains and the polar ice caps spread out to cover far more land than they do today. Even where there were no glaciers and ice caps, the weather became much colder than it had been before. After several thousand years the weather grew warmer again. Then, after another long interval, the glaciers began to advance once

more. This happened several times during the Pleistocene and scientists still do not agree as to why this happened.

Lifestyle of the Woolly Rhinoceros

The Woolly Rhinoceros was specially adapted to the cold conditions of the Pleistocene ice ages. The intensely cold climate meant that much of Europe was stripped of its normal vegetation and tundra spread across the continent. Tundra is the name given to the type of landscape seen in this book. For much of the year the land lay under snow, but during the short Summer, plants grew with amazing speed and vitality. Even so, it was too cold for trees or any other large plant to survive and the tundra was generally flat and monotonous. Landscapes of this kind can be found in northern Canada and Russia today. The Woolly Rhinoceros had many special adaptations to help it survive in such inhospitable conditions. Most noticeable was its shaggy coat which gave it its name. The reddish-brown fur

234

was in two layers to help it keep out the cold. There was a layer of strong, thick hair which was a protection against the bitter wind, even in the depths of Winter. Beneath this was a layer of short, soft fur which was capable of retaining the body warmth of the animal very efficiently. With a total length of just ten feet, the Woolly Rhinoceros was smaller than its ancestors. This meant that it needed less food to survive in the food-scarce tundra. It was also able to store vast reserves of fat under its skin. During the short Summer the Woolly Rhinoceros would eat as much as possible to build up its fat. When Winter brought food shortages the animal could then survive on its fat supply.

Animals of the ice ages

All the animals in the story lived at the same time and in the same place. The Woolly Mammoth is perhaps the best known of these. Like the Woolly Rhinoceros, the Mammoth was a type of animal adapted to a cold climate, though most other Mammoths lived in warmer areas. It had the same two layers of fur as the Woolly Rhinoceros and was also smaller than others of its kind. It is thought that the Mammoth used its tusks to brush aside snow so that it could reach food on the ground. The Megaceros is also known as the Irish Elk, because a lot of its bones have been found in Ireland. It was a gigantic species of deer which had the largest antlers ever to grow on a deer. One set of antlers has been found measuring 12 feet across. The Cave Bear gained its name because scientists found so many of the animals bones in caves. It is believed that Cave Bears hibernated during the long cold Winter, just as modern bears do, and that some died in their dens during the Winter. The Homotherium was the last in a long line of spectacular animals. It was a type of Saber Tooth Cat which somehow managed to survive for thousands of years after the other species became extinct. All these now extinct animals seem to have died out as the last ice age came to a close. Some scientists think this was due to the arrival of warmer weather to which the creatures were not adjusted. Others believe that the spread of man had a lot to do with extinction. Groups of men hunted most of the large plant-eating animals so they may have been hunted to extinction, as almost happened to the American Bison last century. Of all the animals in the story only the Musk Oxen and the wolves still survive. Musk Oxen live in Greenland and northern Canada where tundra still exists, but they are very rare. Wolves were common in most temperate regions until a few hundred years ago. They now survive in remote areas. Man is undoubtedly the most numerous of all the creatures in our story. He has not only survived but thrived.

The adaptations of the Woolly Rhinoceros to a cold climate.

Height: 4½ feet
Length: 10 feet

Thick fur to keep warm

Strong horn for defense

Small size requires less food

Layers of fat to store food

TERMS TO REMEMBER
Dinosaur Terms to Remember

Ankylosaurs — "Fused lizard" dinosaurs with heavy bodies, short limbs and protective armor.

Carnosaurs — Means "flesh lizard"; the large and powerful flesh-eating dinosaurs.

Ceratopsian — "Horned dinosaurs", which were among the last to appear and among the most abundant of all dinosaur groups. A type with large beaks and neck frills.

Coelurosaurs — Means "hollow-tailed lizard"; a group of 16 separate dinosaur families, all of which were small and slightly built.

Mammals — A class of higher vertebrates including man and other animals that nourish their young with milk secreted by mammary glands and are usually more or less covered with hair.

Mesozoic — Comes from the Greek meaning "middle life" and refers to the geologic era between the Paleozoic and the Cenozoic. The Mesozoic is divided into three periods: the Triassic, the Jurassic and the Cretaceous.

Ornithopods — "Bird feet" dinosaurs capable of walking on their back legs.

Ornithischian — One of two families of dinosaur which means "bird-hipped" animal.

Paleontology — The science of dealing with past life from early geologic records and fossil remains.

Prosauropods — Means literally "before the lizard feet" dinosaurs, or Sauropods.

Pterosaurs — Bird-like "winged lizards" which were not dinosaurs at all but a group of animals capable of gliding long distances.

Reptiles — Animals that crawl or move on their belly or on short legs. The body is usually covered with scales or bony plates.

Saurischian — One of two families of dinosaur that means "lizard-hipped" animal.

Sauropods — The family of "lizard-feet" dinosaurs which included some of the largest animals known to have lived.

Stegosaurs — "Roof lizard", or plated dinosaurs with bones or spikes protruding through thick skin.

Thecodontians — Socket-toothed reptiles which first appeared about 230 million years ago and are thought to have given way to the dinosaurs.

Ice Age Terms to Remember

Creodontes
The earliest group of meat-eating mammals. Sharp teeth and a huge head characterized these beasts.

Diatryma
A large, meat-eating bird that was taller than a man. These birds competed with meat-eating mammals for food.

Dinictis
This creature is the ancestor of all cats, both the biting cats—which still exist today (our big jungle cats)—and the now-extinct Saber Tooth cats.

Homotherium
A type of Saber Tooth cat which survived for thousands of years after many other species of cat became extinct.

Ice Age
A period of time within the larger Pleistocene period (2 million years ago-10,000 years ago), during which huge sheets of ice, 2 miles thick in places, covered large portions of the world. Several Ice Ages occurred during the Pleistocene period.

Interglacial
A warming period that occurred between Ice Ages. During these periods the ice that covered much of the world melted, forming new lakes and irrigating new forests.

Megaceros
Also known as the "Irish Elk", since many of its bones have been found in Ireland, this giant deer had antlers that measured up to 12 feet across.

Neanderthal
Primitive man who lived about 100,000 years ago. These were short, ape-like humans who hunted cave bears and other Ice Age animals.

Pleistocene
The period of time on Earth that began 2 million years ago and ended 10,000 years ago. It was during this period that several Ice Ages occurred.

Tar Pit
A pool of liquid formed when oil seeps up from deep underground and collects in a hollow on the surface. Many dinosaurs and Ice Age Creatures were trapped in tar pits, preserving their fossils until the present.